Mysticism In American Literature

Thoreau's Quest
and
Whitman's Self

Paul Hourihan

Edited by Anna Hourihan

Foreword by V. K. Chari

Vedantic Shores Press
Redding, CA

Published by: Vedantic Shores Press,
                P.O. Box 493100
                Redding, CA 96049
                info@vedanticshorespress.com
                http://www.VedanticShoresPress.com

COPYRIGHT © 2004 by Estate of Paul Hourihan.
Printed and bound in the United States of America.

Cover design by Emily Dawidowicz, Fleshcolour New Media
http://www.fleshcolour.com

First Printing 2004

Publisher's Cataloguing-in-Publication
(Provided by Quality Books, Inc.)

Hourihan, Paul,
     Mysticism in American Literature : Thoreau's quest
and Whitman's self / Paul Hourihan ; edited by Anna
Hourihan. — 1st ed.
     p. cm.
     Includes index and bibliographic references.
     LCCN 2003110788
     ISBN 1-931816-03-4

     1. Thoreau, Henry David, 1817–1862—Religion.
2. Whitman, Walt, 1819–1892—Religion. 3. Mysticism in
literature. 4. Religion and literature—United States—
History—19th century. I. Title.

PS3057.R4H68 2004   810.9'382
                           QBI03-200751

Foreword

This study of Thoreau and Whitman is valuable not only as a critical interpretation, but as a deeply insightful "biography" of these two great minds, in charting which Dr. Hourihan brings to his task a certain inwardness of understanding combined with the force of personal conviction. While the contrasting features of Thoreau's and Whitman's temperaments are brought into sharp focus, it is shown that, in their own individual ways, both men had experience, at one time or another, of the ecstasy of being. I agree with his argument that both men were "failed" mystics who could not stabilize their insights. But of course this is so only when we judge them by the highest standards of mystical experience that we know of. The "dual consciousness" or the consciousness of the "I" as a witness ("sakshi" in Vedantic language) did perhaps persist throughout their lives. In Whitman's case, as Karl Shapiro once wrote:

> His leap into the personal infinite, however,
> saved him from drowning in his Susquehanna.

Unfortunately, in our time, the message of these men is all but forgotten. Thoreau urged his countrymen to simplify their lives and turn their minds to the exploration of the self within. "Simplify, simplify," "Explore thyself," "Be expert in home cosmography," he exhorted them. But his "chanticleer" calls have been swept away by the aggressive commercialism and expansionism of our age. It is equally ironic that Whitman's

cosmic self lies decentered, in tatters amid all the contending
idioms and ideologies of modern criticism—new nationalism,
new historicism, deconstruction, gender politics, and so forth.
At a time like this, Dr. Hourihan performs a valuable service
by his courageous reaffirmation of what is of permanent value
in the lives and works of two of the most original minds in
American literature.

– V. K. Chari, Professor Emeritus,
Carleton University, and author of
Whitman in the Light of Vedantic Mysticism

Author's Note

Most of the material used for this volume first appeared as lectures in a course on mysticism given some years ago, and hence the oral influence that still lingers inevitably in many places.

P.H.

My deepest gratitude to Anna Hourihan for her editorial assistance in the preparation of this volume.

P.H.

Contents

Introduction

Mysticism is an experience of the Truth—hence will express itself in countless ways. Literature being one.

Mysticism is described as secret, closed—something is encountered unknown to the ordinary intellect, the confrontation of a new mind ... which was innately there. It is Life—it is Consciousness, the self that we experience in Mysticism—and then become.

But isn't Mysticism ineffable? How can we really discuss it, for what it *is*? The ultimate *samadhi*, the higher union with Godhead, is no doubt beyond our power to communicate or grasp. But Mysticism is not only this supernal peak, it has many levels. It is not only the final gnosis, it is thousands of intermediate experiences—moments, insights, decisions, epiphanies that come to us along the way. It is a whole way of life, with attitudes, motivations, incentives, assumptions that undergird such an existence.

Life is charged everywhere with mystical possibilities ... in art, music, science, literature, the world of the intellect. In ordinary life also. Consider our experience of human love at its best—how profound, how mystical this experience truly is. How "ineffable" also. Mysticism in nature, what we call nature-mysticism—hardly needs to be mentioned. Or the mysticism of childhood and adolescence, the uncanny intuitions that came to us, captured by William Blake in his quatrain:

1

> *To see a World in a Grain of Sand,*
> *And a Heaven in a Wild Flower,*
> *Hold Infinity in the palm of your hand*
> *And Eternity in an hour....*[*]

Henry Thoreau and Walt Whitman were both great American writers and were both mystics, but they are instructive for our purpose in certain other ways.

They were born within a two-year period (Thoreau in 1817, Whitman in 1819); they knew and admired the other's work and met personally in 1856; they came to public notice for the first time (1854–1855) within a year of each other; both were familiar with the Hindu scriptures, and acknowledged R. W. Emerson as their mentor and chief early influence (Thoreau in close continued personal contact, Whitman from a distance through the written word). Historically they stand as two preeminent originals in American Literature in their century.

Further, they offer a fascinating study in contrasts. Their personalities and viewpoints are opposite in almost every respect so that in examining them we gain insight into two diametrically opposed alternatives to the life of regeneration.

In both their cases we know much about their inner development as well as their writings. We have their journals and personal letters, which give us a psychological as well as literary approach to them, an understanding of the biography of their *minds* as well as of their bodies. For us, the writings become an index to the more important matter of their spiritual journey. In their case, and perhaps with every great man, the outer works are only a footnote to the true story that is going on, which is the evolution of his spirit, the gradual manifestation of his true self. If he's a writer and seeking truth, his works will be revealing milestones along the way, enlightening us about much more than his literary progress.

We should study them in detail.

---

[*] From the poem "Auguries of Innocence"

• • •

Since the focus of the present volume is mysticism, two aspects of Thoreau's *Walden* will be passed over. One is its interpretation of nature. True nature lovers read *Walden* from that standpoint, which doesn't much concern us. It seems incidental to the mysticism. Another is the social criticism which flows through everything Thoreau writes. Too much time won't be spent on that either. This is, again, a phase of his creatureliness. He is aware of evils in the world and criticizes them, just as he is a naturalist, observing trees, lakes and wildlife—expressions of his earthly personality, whereby he fills the time with congenial activities or writings, but behind them all is the spiritual theme, the life of the potential mystic, with which we will be mostly concerned.

Thoreau's Quest

Rather than love, than money, than fame, give me truth.

—Henry David Thoreau,
Walden, "Conclusion"

Henry David Thoreau

Henry Thoreau (1817–1862) is an archetypal figure. We have lived lives like his—or will. His is a universal quest pursued with fervent single-mindedness to pluck out from the heart of the universe the secret of its mystery. Alone—with no guru (Emerson disappointed him grievously because of his *esthetic* approach to life), no encouragement.

Thoreau is the grimly serious, impassioned, defiant young man who sets out on a pilgrimage to discover the meaning of life and is determined to let nothing stand in his way. He seeks to achieve perfection.

He becomes a pilgrim to himself—to his new self, to the life he has resolved to bring into being. He wants to discover all the possibilities of becoming new-born and to report his findings back to men. As he will do in *Walden*.

The journals he wrote in his early twenties anticipate the themes and spirit of his famous autobiography and reflect his first stirrings of spiritual hunger. From the outset we note this craving for the transcendental, for mystical knowledge. To begin with, his need for solitude:

> I only ask a clean seat. I will build my lodge on the southern slope of some hill and take there the life the gods send me…. It will be success if I shall have left myself behind.[1]

It is the ego-self, the creature-consciousness, that he recognizes as the enemy. All his short life (he died at 44) he was struggling against it in this sharp, clear knowledge ... although sometimes, in hating *it,* he will turn his anger against *men* and their world.

People seemed to be living, he wrote, but are really dead. Even his once-esteemed mentor, Ralph Waldo Emerson, lived a shadow life. As he himself did. He did not exclude himself in the general fall. *How can he awake?* His two years at Walden was his attempt to awaken himself with his own hands.

Thoreau had met his fellow Concordian, Emerson, in 1837 when Henry, native to their town, was graduating from Harvard. It was more than a decade before Thoreau discovered that Emerson, his guru, fourteen years his senior, was strictly an academic-intellectual in his approach to the high and urgent matters of spiritual realization.

Emerson was surrounded by an aura of expectation and eminence from his early days, and when his first essays were published they were so unique in their style, so electrifying in their insight, that people felt, here at last was the American sage they had been waiting for. It took Thoreau, enthralled by the older man's grace and brilliance, almost a dozen years before he realized that Emerson was not serious about living the principles he could expound with such eloquence, and that he was only an intellectual in these deep and vital waters of the soul. He could write about them with rare understanding, but essentially like a man describing an illness or a condition he has never had himself. He masters all the symptoms but never really experiences it, never takes that drink of alcohol, that drug, or that spiritual ecstasy, knowing about it only from hearsay.

Henry Thoreau begins his journal in 1837, on Emerson's urging, and the first two books through 1845 are the most valuable sections of it. They are an anticipation of *Walden* itself. Restive during his middle twenties, he goes to Walden at twenty-eight and completes his sojourn there by the time he is thirty. He rewrites his book seven times in the next seven years, becoming the most self-conscious of writers. Everyone knows his work is a highly finished product—no one writes prose like this spontaneously. It is an intensely and carefully wrought achievement.

It was coolly, blandly received—the worst kind of response for Thoreau. The year after its publication (1854) occurs a depression that lasted for more than a year, compelling us to infer a direct relationship, at least in part, between the two events. Anyone who rewrites a work seven times, putting his soul's experience into it, and then finds it indifferently noticed by his contemporaries, may not take it kindly. He was neither vindicated by rejection, nor seduced by acclaim. A pall of *indifference* hung over the work year after year, although a few of course—there are always the discerning few—discovered it for what it was.

No one could understand the strange depression which seized him. Doctors examined him and all kinds of advice was given, but no one explained it. Nor has any biographer done so. His two chief interpreters have simply pointed it out as a mysterious thing. A puzzle indeed it is: a man of great energy, will, vitality, succumbs to this demoralizing condition for reasons no one can supply. He gradually works out of it—but never completely.

Emerson invited him to live at his house as a possible help. Years before, Thoreau had spent two years at the master's house, but Emerson, now the villain, was himself one of the forces that Thoreau felt dragging him into lethargy and disillusionment.

His last years are marked by a compulsive naturalism. It was an effort merely to keep going, to return to the scene of his conquest—his *self*-conquest—at Walden Pond. Now he goes not as a devotee of nature's secrets but as a man who does this to pass the time. Hence his journals of these last few years, from the man who wrote *Walden,* are tedious to read. There is book after book of impersonal scrutiny of Nature, which has hardly any of the insights and beauty we would expect from Henry Thoreau, indicating that he has lost something priceless and is simply going on the best way he can. When he caught cold in 1860 the germs seized an organism geared for decline (the depression of 1855 a clue). The cold advanced to pneumonia, which led in turn to tuberculosis, in that age an all but incurable disease.

We see the high point of his life, then, is 1847 when he leaves Walden. He holds this balance for a few years thereafter. The journals of that period are full of a vigor and self-confidence based on the purifying disciplines of the two-year Walden period. This was also a time when he begins to show his anger at society and at Emerson in particular. One of his best essays is called, significantly, "Life Without Principle," a bitter title, aimed at none other than Emerson.

For a few more years he approximates the level he had achieved at Walden, works hard on the book in the expectation that it will bring him at least some acknowledgment. But by submitting the book to his fellows he had provided himself a never-ending store of self-reproach with the realization that shamelessly, unaccountably, he had revealed his innermost life for the examination and approval of people for whom he had expressed so often elemental scorn and impatience. Was the problem Emerson or Thoreau? Had he not made his own bed of misery?

The fact also that he was not married, that he lacked an intimate source of support and strength, may well have been a factor in the wretchedness that harassed him. The right kind of woman, such as William Blake, for example, had found, would have given him an additional, badly needed source of inspiration. Thoreau always had to dig it out of himself, or out of nature; and nature had become less and less responsive to his moods.

What we bring to nature, we find there. She is a kind of wish-fulfilling tree. Whatever gift we offer her, she responds appropriately. If we bring nothing, she is dead. If we bring an illumined spirit, she seems a vehicle of the divine—as she had been in Walden. The Nature that Thoreau had discovered in his early years makes us all go out to that same Nature, those woods and lakes, looking for those insights, and find them not. The insights were self-generated by Thoreau, though Nature in her silence and solitude had provided him the neutral territory in which to discover himself.

But he wasn't experiencing these insights a few years later— only the depths of fields, the widths of trees, the various species of birds and animals: naturalism without the mystical content. His decline sets in slowly and when the infection seizes his organism he had no resistance to it. He was ready to die.

He felt, apparently, that he had reached the highest spiritual point he was going to achieve in this life sometime around the early 1850s and perhaps, as we have conjectured, at Walden itself in 1847. But he was occupied with the writing and tireless rewriting of the book, in the following six or seven years: reenacting the experience of those two years endlessly, recapturing its uniqueness. When he began to run out of momentum, new hope that the secret of life might yet be discovered, there were those two paragon years he could look back on, drawing emotional dividends from the recollection.

He was like a parent reliving his youth in the youth of his children. *Walden* gave Thoreau a chance to relive his hour of greatness, when that hour had passed. Through 1854 when he is thirty-seven he has the benefit of the actual and then of the remembered perfection of Walden. He pours his soul into the book, which fails to dazzle the world, heightening his conviction that what the mass of men call good he believed in his soul to be bad, plunging him—along with his acute and continuing disillusion-ment at Emerson, self-described as "the word-man"—into his depression.

If one conceives of a man as not having a soul but rather a body, mind, and ego, depressions can be analyzed psychologically and often alleviated or removed with the help of certain therapies. But if one conceives of a man as having a soul, as being a soul, and his body, organs, ego, senses, and his mind, its instruments, then the depression of any man of relative spiritual advancement will always have a spiritual base.

If we *are* souls, if our nature—as the mystics tell us—is divine at bottom, then depression will be connected in some way, directly or indirectly, with our failure to realize, to remember, or to live for this truth. It will be in some way or other an identification with the non-divine, with the falseness. So it was with Thoreau.

He identified emotionally with such phenomena as the publication of his book, the flawed character of Ralph Waldo Emerson, the lives his contemporaries were leading, and so forth. He may have been right about these and other matters but as a spiritual aspirant of considerable development he should have been beyond their reach. It is not easy to do this. But in Henry David Thoreau we are studying a potentially great soul, someone who can teach us how to live, not remind us of our ordinary weaknesses. The great soul is supposed to be beyond others. Whatever happens to him—whether his book is accepted or not—should be immaterial to him.

So the depression came. He had struggled to achieve knowledge, to tap the mystery of things, to find out what the essence of life was, what the truth of himself was, had done all this as far as he could, and then seemed unable to maintain the edge of his will to continue with more struggle.

The depression is a symptom of his self-division, of his failure to be true to the Walden awakenings. He failed to read his own book, neglected to take to heart the lessons he was trying to impress on others on being true to the insights of their finest hours and having their whole life built around that realization, about God being with us if we could only open the channel and instantly feel the divine presence. These and similar ideas, which pervade the book, he was unable to embody in his own life. Hence his soul succumbs to ego-consciousness, to his creature-weaknesses, to depression.

In the struggle to change, and to become something closer to what we truly wish to be, depression is for all of us a pitfall. A

preeminent spiritual instructor in India, a swami, was discussing
spiritual matters with a group of young monks in his care; they
were asking him basic questions about the problems in spiritual
life. These were young men of renunciation and we would expect
him to give them some special kind of knowledge, emphasizing
the weaknesses of the flesh perhaps, or some teaching appropriate
to monasticism. One of them asked: "What is the principal
difficulty in spiritual life?"—Spiritual life of course being the life
of regeneration that Thoreau was leading at Walden. Here was the
swami's chance to say something unforgettable to the monks. He
was esteemed as a renowned spiritual trainer of his time so that
anything he said at this point would have been remembered—some
counsel that would apply to each of them irrespective of different
backgrounds and capacities. Was there any one thing that would affect
them equally as the primary obstacle in spiritual life? He thought a
moment and then said: "Don't let your minds give in to depression."

The obstacle. More important than any of the deadly sins we
might think of—without exception it applies to all of us as well.
He might have mentioned one or two others but this he chose as
being obviously the chief difficulty.

Depression is the experience we feel at every step of genuine
development. After a stage of advance is made in spiritual life,
depression is the potential result. There will always be this tendency
of the organism to sink back to the level it occupied prior to the
advance. If we are not aware of the phenomenon, when the
depression comes upon us, we feel there is something special
happening to us. We look for psychological patterns to explain
it—in our family, our marriage, our job, our background. Sometimes, of course, these areas do contribute. But, even in a person
with an ideal upbringing, who has no problems with his wife or
with his associates, who nevertheless is leading a life aimed at
discovering his spirituality, his inner truth, will undergo these
depressions recurrently, no matter who it is, whether monk or
householder, male or female. This is the one thing we have in

common, except that when it comes upon us it is like the disease of influenza, which is not usually fatal but which demoralizes and enervates—depression is like an influenza of the spirit. We wonder what is causing it—why am I in this state?

It is the price we pay for being human; and then, being human, seeking the divine. If we are content to be merely human these depressions are minimal or can usually be explained in psychological terms. But if we are struggling to discover who we are and seeking the divine essence within, depression is our habitual lot.

It is the proof that we are progressing. If there are no depressions in our lives, we have not advanced. For every hill there will be a valley, for every rise a trough. Depressions are these troughs and valleys of spiritual life. Wherever there is a rise in nature, they will appear—in the inner landscape also. Wherever there is a rise there will have to be a sinking back—this is the compulsion of the metabolism. Perhaps only in the rare saint is there comparatively a direct line forward. But even in the lives of saints we read about their dark nights of the soul: a dramatic description of depressions we all meet inescapably on the path.

If we could realize what their implications really are we would gain a kind of grim satisfaction, as though to remind ourselves that they wouldn't have appeared if we weren't struggling to go beyond ourselves. If I was content with what I have been, these depressions will be minor and brief. If I've attempted to achieve perfection, as Thoreau did at Walden, if I've attempted to make myself complete and pure, as he came close to the threshold of doing, glimpsing the country that beckoned just beyond—and *then* begin to sink back, depression will be unavoidable and potent.

Unfortunately he didn't have a mystical background to support him, which is part of our problem today as well. Thoreau and Whitman were both unchurched and had no spiritual tradition in which to function. They were both Protestants also, and although Protestantism has produced some valuable things, including the great hymns, it lacks a strong mystical orientation.

Hence, Thoreau and Whitman, as Protestants, are at a loss when they discover their mystical leanings. Where will they turn for the immediate and traditional support which is open to the Hindu, the Buddhist, the Catholic, the Sufi, who discovers in himself the same tendency? The Protestant is at a disadvantage.

But wherever there is disadvantage there will be compensations. If you have to do everything yourself, you may do more than anyone else. Thoreau seems to be potentially that kind of seeker. He had to do it all himself. No tradition, no teacher. Emerson was a literary teacher, not a spiritual one, the kind that Thoreau really craved and needed.

Had he known a spiritual man when this depression came, it could have been explained as an inevitable part of what he was doing and in fact as a good omen—as a sign that he had already advanced far beyond his expectations, the depression being the weight of Nature, of his past self embodying that Nature, trying to reclaim its lost territory. Thoreau didn't seem to grasp this, instead identified with the depression and never decisively pulled out of it.

So we have in him a life of great spiritual promise, a potential saint, who misses the goal and then fades away. Fortunately he recovered something on his deathbed. His faith in spirit, in the prospects of self-realization, returned at the end. When people came to console him, he did the consoling. There was no self-pity—everything calm, serene, reconciled. Everyone noticed that a strange radiance filled the room. What he had at Walden was distilled again in those last few weeks. Nevertheless—though his life is a success, certainly—there is a feeling of frustration and loss about it too.

Something to instruct and yet something to warn us. When we get depressed we should see it in perspective. We mustn't feel that we are being sought out or that we are worthless creatures. This condition, for someone struggling to spiritualize his nature, will be recurrent. If we can view it in that light we won't be put off, will be more patient with ourselves—and with critics when they complain about us.

• • •

Thoreau is one of the Transcendentalists. Transcendentalism is Romanticism in America. In the Romantic Movement the individual emerged as the center of literary, creative, and philosophical contemplation. Man the unknown, the spiritual personality, was first sighted and celebrated by the Romantics as a group. Never before was this done in the West. So the movement is extremely important—equally important as the Renaissance, perhaps more so.

The Romantics first saw man as potentially what the mystics of all time had always said he was. They saw with a new perspective, which accounts for the luster emanating from the poetry of Keats and Shelley and the others, despite their often self-conscious posturings. We feel that there is a special quality about them and we don't know what it is: it is that.

They are celebrating the divine in man to the best of their ability. The revelation has come to them and it is the truth of their discovery that irradiates their work. Only one or two of them—in fact, only Blake really—knew consciously what it was all about. The others were merely reflectors of themselves from their own intuitions. The insights were greater than they were. Like many mystics before and after them, they couldn't live up to the truth of the revelations, which they thought were coming to them from beyond and which they captured in chosen moments. Wordsworth, Shelley, Emerson, they all felt this. It isn't so. The insights are from the inner realm, from the soul.

The world was calling for the new age, hence it wasn't left to an individual mystic or particular poet in isolated solitude to announce the urgent truths. Whole groups of artists—in England, and in North America a generation later, on the Continent as well: Goethe and Schiller in Germany, Chateaubriand and others in France—were being called upon to make these radical insights, these revolutionary conceptions of man's nature, irrevocably available, introducing them into the thought-stream of humanity, never to depart again.

We often hastily identify the Romantic Movement with moonlight, mystery, theatrical escapism from the "real world," but it is not that, though it has that fringe aspect. There were minor Romantics. There were Gothic novelists, poets of fantasy and melodrama. But the major Romantics are seers, mystics potentially and their movement is the most momentous we can discern in Western history. Other progressive developments of history can be seen as leading up to that and have been only tentative. Even the Renaissance faded into the rationalistic enlightenment of the eighteenth century.

With Romanticism we come to modern times and a new voice for mankind. People in 1800 were thinking like people in 2000, almost from one year to the next, with an electrifying change. In 1790 they are thinking the way man always has: God is in his heaven and man is here on earth, and either there is no God or else man is a kind of sinner to whom God will show his blessings, perhaps in heaven—this older view. All that changes. Their tone is our tone. It is introspective, psychological, personal, intimate, spiritual, free, marked by the themes we think of as essentially modern.

Especially the theme of the individual in all his aspects—of little or no concern to men before that, but with the Romantics the individual occupies the center of the stage and has been there basically ever since. This has had its drawbacks and difficulties. It has resulted in much anarchy, rioting, and tumult, but it is the price we pay for the necessity of this enthronement of man at the heart of the universe. Not man in his weaknesses and mortal limitations, but the Blakean man, the apocalyptic man, potentially the Christ man. The man the Romantics discovered.

Transcendentalism carries the discovery over into America, takes the Romantic Experience and philosophizes, idealizes, about it. It has two or three basic ideas that are in Thoreau, who becomes a part of the group. It is hard to say how he would have fared without this background. It wasn't exactly a tradition (earlier we noted that he lacked such) but was at least an intellectual framework. It gave him a sanction and encouragement during his early years in his hopes for his life.

Emerson's writings and *Walden* itself are the best literary expression of Transcendentalism. The Transcendentalists said there were ideas *innately* in man, that he had the power to experience truth beyond the reach of the senses and the intellect; hence there was a possibility of direct revelation into the heart of truth itself. They glorified the mind and soul, rejecting the mechanistic philosophies of the eighteenth century. Theirs was a new idealism, a philosophy in which something in man *transcends* the figure provided to us in previous ages. There is a divine faculty, a power in man, independent of the senses and the intellect. In Nature, they said, we can find ourselves more fully than in society because Nature will give us her truth in an unconscious, unmediated guise. One of man's problems is to elevate and perfect these organic inspirations of Nature. In Nature's presence—in solitude, in silence, in communion with the earth—he may discover these inner promptings.

Epitomizing all of this is the image of Henry Thoreau at Walden Pond flashing across our imaginations with an immortal impact.

Transcendentalists also tended to believe in reincarnation. Such a spiritual presence as the soul could not fulfill itself in one lifetime; to realize its potentialities it needed many. For the first time in American history we find a good many thinkers, notably Emerson and his circle, all at once believing and writing about this. Thoreau certainly did. In *Walden* we see the theme permeating the work. He doesn't make it explicit but it clearly has become part of him.

These were some of the motifs of transcendentalism, essentially a spiritual movement, a philosophy of mysticism. Thoreau, however, wanted to embody this philosophy in actual life. Most of its adherents talked about it beautifully or wrote about it, as Emerson did. But from our earliest glimpse of Thoreau he was possessed by an existentialist approach to the problem of the self.

If there was a soul it had to be realized, otherwise it was only a concept, a metaphysical expression. Not to experience something within man's reach, *of that nature,* seemed an obnoxious and almost criminal act—hence his increasing alienation from the other transcendentalists when he discovered that they, like most men, were perfectly willing to confine their inspirations to art and literature.

Even in his early journals, at this period of 1837–42 when he's beginning to think of Walden, when it is little more than a dream, there are a hundred passages reflecting the same spirit we will find animating *Walden* itself:

> We are constantly invited to be what we are; as to something worthy and noble....[2]

> Even the wisest and the best are apt to use their lives as the occasion to do something else in than to live greatly. But we should hang as fondly over this work as the finishing and embellishment of a poem.[3]

Emerson, the thinker, spent his time polishing his essays and poems, but for Thoreau the true poem was the life of the self. What could surpass this? We should treat our own lives as a work of art, and that is all we have to do. How to live—to make each day like a canvas the artist paints and to do it as well as we can. This insight he never lost. The work of self-culture, *his* work. "There is but one obligation, and that is the obligation to obey the highest dictate. None can lay me under another which would supersede this."[4]

But, in fact, he consumed too much time with *Walden.* Those seven drafts were a contradiction of this statement of belief. Not that we expect a rough and careless presentation, but the great seers and mystics didn't revise their work in this manner. We don't find them *polishing* their essays in the Emersonian manner.

Does this mean that Thoreau is not a genuine seer? It means that in *that* respect he was on the wrong track, descending to mere literature. In comparison to what he had seen and was capable of, it becomes a turning away from those heights. As a result we have a classic work of literature. But from the point of view of Thoreau's own life, it was a mistake. Those hundreds of hours of revision were on a much lower level, that of mundane existence.

Again, not that we aren't grateful for *Walden* and its incandescent prose, its masterly quality. But for our purposes it is Thoreau's *life*, his mystical insights and spiritual development that may be more instructive than anything he wrote. We are chiefly interested in the *man* in this work. Not the masterpiece itself. Of course, it is a good way to pass your time perfecting a literary jewel, but, spiritually speaking, it was mistaken. He becomes embroiled in the endeavor and loses the glow and edge of his experiences, becomes a purveyor of them in the form of a book. It would have been better had he written it once and said, I have other things to do now, other lives to live.

He didn't take this approach because obviously he wanted recognition. It was his life's work. It was *his* contribution to the world's intellectual culture. From *our* standpoint we may not have wanted it otherwise. But from *his*? And his is really our deepest standpoint too, because we are him. As we study a Thoreau, we see more and more that his is an archetypal life enabling us to see ourselves in him, and although we are glad of the rare fruit of his labor, still, we had rather have him succeed spiritually and achieve illumination to some substantial degree—then, we could have seen ourselves doing the same thing.

Another passage from those early journals which form the nucleus of *Walden:* "I would be as clean as ye, o woods. I shall not rest till I be as innocent as you."[5]

This is not the innocence of childhood, but an *enlightened* innocence. One is the innocence of nature, one the innocence of the soul. One is given, one achieved—by overcoming. "Nature," he will tell us, "is hard to be overcome, but she must be overcome."[6] The innocence he seeks is to be won by discipline, by struggle. *It is the discipline that purifies us.* It won't be given. The purity is there, no doubt—innate, self-existent. It is the struggle of spiritual life that removes the impurities covering it. As a chemist removes the impurities from water. Thoreau is a chemist to himself: *"I shall not rest...."*

"The brave man does not mind the call of the trumpet—nor the idle clashing of swords without, for the infinite din within."[7] Din is the chaos of many inner voices. The brave man is the spiritual man. For Thoreau there is only one brave man—he who struggles with himself. This man ignores the agitation of his contemporaries because he hears another sound, another music, within.

"War is but a training compared with the active service of *his* peace"—recalling William James' moral equivalent of war. How can we capture that sense of selfless dedication that the soldier manifests on the battlefield and, in consequence, is taken out of himself in the experience of a new identity? How, asked James, can we do that in peacetime? Thoreau has an answer: the life of spiritual regeneration.

James himself missed this discovery. Like Emerson, he was an investigator into possibilities for *others* to know. Yet minds like James' and Emerson's are necessary too—those who have no plans to incorporate into their lives these struggles, who write so eloquently about the underlying principles but make no effort to implement them in their own characters. If it weren't for them we wouldn't have these mappings of the spiritual life and its potentialities. Someone has to formulate them and then declare: you be the hero I can only describe. You be my vicarious self-realization, Henry Thoreau—says Emerson, in so many words. This is not to fault them, it is simply to see them as playing a role that is limited—and then the Thoreaus, the Blakes, respond. Without their clarion calls, the latter might not have made the struggle in earnest.

"—Is he not at war, the brave man?" Already at twenty-four Thoreau had undergone a spiritual awakening. He was no longer the once-born man of peace, like Emerson. He was a man at war with himself, Walden his attempt to resolve the problem and to gain spiritual clarity and serenity.

Before he went to Walden his reputation was that of a difficult young man with a fondness for shocking epigrams and then walking out on the company. Already in evidence during those years was the hard kernel of scorn for his contemporaries, for the ways of Concord, the lifestyles of his fellow men. He didn't associate in general with others, felt superior to them. His earlier journals were marked and marred by this contempt for men.

When Whitman met Thoreau in 1856 they were both impressed with each other. But Whitman was disappointed to discover this element in Thoreau. They walked up Broadway, the crowded Manhattan thoroughfare, Whitman was in his element, Thoreau making comments on people passing by—they seemed asleep, still in animal form. Whitman was disappointed and later made the penetrating comment that Henry Thoreau didn't seem to understand how individual men actually are and how anyone could be different from him.

This wasn't the whole Thoreau, however. If we read his letters, for instance, particularly his personal messages to a few disciples who came to him after Walden, we realize there was another sleeping, hidden part of him. But he never completely weeded out the scornfulness, which of course would have contributed to his depression.

As long as there is a large element of egoism, depression will be recurrent. Perhaps it is the presence of this ego-self along with the spirit, the two together that produces the depression. The fact that we can have so much shadow-haunted ego-consciousness despite all our years of struggle in our Walden adventures, and all our meditations and studies, can be discouraging. It disheartened Thoreau. When will we throw off this thing keeping us from our destiny? How are we going to do it? We struggle as none of our contemporaries are struggling, do things they aren't capable of; often have insights far beyond theirs. Certainly this was true of

Thoreau. Again, the archetype: in him we see ourselves. The best of us is in him. And yet, despite all this, he can't shake off the burden. The spectre clings.

Still, he comes from Walden changed. Many people noticed the humility that was not there before. People who heard him lecture in 1840 and then around 1850 noticed the change. He seemed—different. The word *pure* is constantly coming to people's lips, men and women alike, in their descriptions of Thoreau. There was a purity about him. Not only the fact that he was celibate. That isn't the same thing. You can be married and be pure. It is chasteness of spirit, an inner holiness, that some people emanate. The way of life is secondary. Thoreau had that. So he was changed. Walden did purify him. It gave him a great deal. It didn't however root out enough of his unshakable residue of disdain, which so puzzled Whitman.

"—Does he not resist the ocean swell within him and walk as gently as the summer sea?" The ocean swell within is the seething subconscious world dominated by the ego, attempting to seize the mind of the awakened personality. Most people never know what this ocean swell is—they are what we call once-born. The twice-born person is he who awakens the depths within and then has to learn to dominate the swelling tumult.

That is why St. Paul went to Arabia after his experience on the road to Damascus, overwhelmed by the instantaneous new birth that had come to him. Previously he had been a brilliant once-born character, but after his Damascus road illumination the energies of his subconscious mind were in upheaval, and suddenly, unless he mastered the chaos, he was in danger of losing his sanity. In his case the great psychic explosion came instantly and it took him three years in Arabian solitude to accomplish his purpose, to clarify and subdue his traumatized mind, and then complete the process of the second birth.

This is what Thoreau is referring to when he writes: "Does he not resist the ocean swell within him?" And—as part of his discipline—"walk as gently as the summer sea?" Hence we are enjoined to act peacefully with all men—otherwise we will reawaken the surging tides of blind nature and defeat our own progress.

It wasn't enough for him to do this at home. During these years he was living with his parents, his sisters, and many female boarders, in a large house in an atmosphere of endless gossip, and he had little chance of privacy. He decided he would need a prolonged exposure of solitude to fulfill his dream—the same reason that Saul of Tarsus went to Arabia for those three years, and "conferred not with flesh and blood." So Walden became Thoreau's Arabia. Not so extremely, however. He wasn't a complete recluse, although that is the image he presents to us. Almost every day he returned to his mother's house for a substantial home-cooked meal.

Thoreau's poem "Inspiration"[8] records the phenomenon, written in the same period as the journal excerpts we have examined. He has had a spiritual awakening in the previous weeks. Now he walks alone in the woods, feeling reborn.

> *I hearing get, who had but ears,*
> *And sight, who had but eyes before;*
> *I moments live, who lived but years,*
> *And truth discern, who knew but*
> *learning's lore.*

Before, he heard and saw with sense organs and a once-born mind. Now he hears with an inner power, sees with an inner mind. The moments of inspiration he now lives are eternal; they have a timeless reality, whereas up to this time he has merely lived *years*. These moments that he lives now seem to be so much longer, like the pulse of the eternal. And what he has known before in the way of knowledge is only book-learning. Now he discerns the truth itself.

> *I hear beyond the range of sound,*
> *I see beyond the range of sight,*
> *New earths and skies and seas around,*
> *And in my day the sun doth pale his*
> *light.*

He himself has written a revealing commentary on these two stanzas:

> I see, smell, taste, hear, feel, that everlasting Something to which we are allied, at once our maker, our abode, our destiny, our very Selves; the one historic truth, the most remarkable fact which can become the distinct and uninvited subject of our thought, the actual glory of the universe....[9]

> Our present senses are but the rudiments of what they are destined to become. We are comparatively deaf and dumb and blind, and without smell or taste or feeling. Every generation makes the discovery that its divine vigor has been dissipated, and each sense and faculty misapplied and debauched. The ears were made, not for such trivial uses as men are wont to suppose, but to hear celestial sounds. The eyes were not made for such groveling uses as they are now put to and worn out by, but to behold beauty now invisible. May we not *see* God? ... Surely we are provided with senses as well fitted to penetrate the spaces of the real, the substantial, the eternal, as these outward are to penetrate the material universe.[10]

"—And in my day the sun doth pale his light"—seems like pure rhetorical exaggeration but the idea is confirmed by all mystics, that after their experience the light of the sun loses its power—even if we consider a nonmystical kind of saint, like Thérèse of Lisieux, the French girl who wanted to enter a convent all her short life and died there at the age of twenty-four. She takes what she calls the path of the Little Way. In the course of this yoga she obviously has a mystical revelation and in her autobiography writes that "after what I have experienced all the suns and stars and the whole universe seem insignificant to my own soul." And Thoreau, although he failed of the culminative experience of mysticism, as we infer from his life as a whole, has known part of it and as a result in the new day that dawns "the sun doth pale his light."

How does it come? Suddenly—"more swift its bolt than

lightning is." The kingdom of heaven, says Christ, comes like a thief in the night. For him the kingdom was the awakening of a spiritual consciousness in the mystical experience and it is to this moment that Thoreau makes reference.

The next stanza crystallizes the poem's real meaning:

> *Then chiefly is my natal hour,*
> *And only then my prime of life,*
> *Of manhood's strength it is the flower,*
> *Tis peace's end and war's beginning strife.*

Although his mother's womb gave him one birth he has no life now except in these burning mystical hours. As he has said, "I moments live, who lived but years." This has given him his true birth; only *then* does he know what joy, what the prime of life is.

It is also the end of peace. But what about that state the mystics write of—the peace that passes understanding?—"Tis peace's end and war's beginning strife." It means he is just beginning on the new path. We leave the peace of once-born tranquillity behind— *that* peace is gone forever. We enter into the path grappling with ourselves, our subconscious minds, our inherited characters, and with the external counterparts of these eternal realities—but the main struggle is within. It is the end of that early peace, the peace of Nature. And the war begins. The war we have heard about— war's "beginning strife." *Later*—after the experience of the mystical consciousness, after we have negotiated the passage through chaos—comes that peace that passes understanding.

We perceive the universal character of his life: a young man who had had a spiritual awakening, trying to find a pattern of living to make the revelation assimilable and a part of his substance.

According to Carl Jung, an archetype is a perpetually recurring type of human experience. Henry Thoreau is a classic archetype of the young man who burns with the ardor of self-realization and will let nothing stand in his way as he sets out on this lonely journey within. The saint-in-the-making: this is Henry Thoreau.

As we all are. But he is closer than most of us. Or with more strength and perhaps more vision, and development than most of us have. Yet his weaknesses are perceptibly ours; his strengths potentially ours as well. And the almost desperate courage of his life can only strengthen *us* in our moments of self-indulgence when we feel we can accomplish our goal by reading and thinking about these things. Those moods of passive receptivity have their place, but we have to do more, surely.

We have to discipline ourselves to some extent and practice *some* austerities. For this purpose Thoreau's life is unique and invigorating: its heroic contours make us feel we can do something too—renounce, deny—make us feel we are disciplining our lives.

Part of his problem was the need to gather psychic strength to support him in the early days of the Walden experiment. In Thoreau's case the most temperamentally suitable way was to defy his contemporaries, criticize them, and build up a backlog of nourished resentment and disdain to fortify himself against the internal struggle to come. Regrettable or not, this is what he felt he had to do and in his place we might have done something similar. At the beginning we have to get strength somewhere. But, at first, the only way that Thoreau knows is to declare that what they are doing was wrong and mistaken and he won't live that way, separating himself conspicuously from them and girding his mind with the strength of rejection.

"Everywhere," he writes, "in shops, and offices, and fields, the inhabitants have appeared to me to be doing penance in a thousand remarkable ways." As he looks at his Concord fellows, he thinks that the way they are living proves they can't be in earnest. His irony and wit, which bubbles all through his work, always contains a serious measure of reflection and insight. In the same vein he adds that "The twelve labors of Hercules were trifling in comparison with those which my neighbors have undertaken."[11]

He doesn't let his readers off entirely; in his attempt to win them over he is anything but graceful. "It is very evident what

mean and sneaking lives many of you live," he tells them. This is
part of Thoreau's self-image in private life and he carries it over
into his writing. But that is how he was as a youth. People expected
this kind of remark from him and we see that the persona even
now still clings to him. It is admittedly effective but one wishes he
could have approached his mysticism without the superadded
scorn as a necessary component: "… seeking to curry favor, to get
custom … lying, flattery…." To the reader, no less. No wonder he
had so few of them while he lived.

> I sometimes wonder if we can be so frivolous ... as to
> attend to the gross … form of servitude called Negro
> Slavery….

This was the Abolitionist period. Emerson and others were
all taken up with the thought of removing slavery from the
American life-blood. Thoreau was sympathetic with the cause but
played little role: it was, he said, an irrelevant slavery for the brave
man, for the truly seeing man. For those who don't know of any
other slavery, let them attend to that; but there is another one that
grips us all: "—There are so many keen and subtle masters that
enslave both North and South…. Talk of a divinity in man! Look
at the teamster on the highway…. How godlike, how immortal is
he?" This is the slavery we should be concerned about, the one
that puts us into bondage to our weaknesses, sluggishness, ignorance, and denies that we have any other destiny. "The mass of
men," he concludes gloomily, "lead lives of quiet desperation."

The theme of Man the Unknown engages him, reflecting the
Romantic and Transcendentalist preoccupation: do we really know
what man is? The man we received from our ancestors, from our
religions, cultural and intellectual traditions—this is not man as
he truly is. Thoreau vigorously espoused a new concept: "But man's
capacities have never been measured; nor are we to judge of what
he can do by any precedents, so little has been tried." We have
simply taken things as nature has given them to us and called that
human nature. So little *has* been tried. Thoreau wants to forge

other roads into the psyche, to explore new territories for humanity, and then give us a report of what he has found—setting out on his mission without any encouragement. Emerson gave him land for the hut but nothing more.

"The greater part of what my neighbors call good, I believe in my soul to be bad—" summarizes the pervading mood of these pages. "How vigilant we are! Determined not to live by faith if we can avoid it.... denying the possibility of change." He wants to remake himself and then announce to the world what a man can do.

He reads in the scriptures of the Orient at this time, finding a deep sense of kinship with the sages of the *Bhagavad Gita* and the *Upanishads*. They seem to speak directly to him, and he becomes the first American to respond with such existential empathy to the spirit of these sacred texts. Emerson had introduced him to them but had failed to imbibe their true essence, had regarded them, he said, as wonderful "rhetorical" treatises, as essentially esthetic experiences. But Thoreau saw them as road maps leading to the realization of what man really was, and is constantly quoting them in his works.

In discussing the ancient philosophers of Greece and Asia, he finds it remarkable that we, with our materialistic psychologies, know as much about them as we do—amazing that we have any kind of sympathy or understanding, at all, of what they were talking about.

What is a philosopher? The Western definition is not Thoreau's: "To be a philosopher ... [is] to love wisdom ... to live a life of simplicity.... It is to solve some of the problems of life." For the West as a whole, however, a philosopher is mainly a man of thought, an analyst, a systematizer. But like Thomas Aquinas, who had a personal experience of the truth and was unable afterwards to continue his philosophizing, Thoreau draws a distinction between the Western concept of a philosopher and what he might actually be: a man who has experienced the reality he theorizes about in his theological moments.

It is a vital distinction. Plato's allegory of the cave[12] has dramatized this for all time—the two types of mind. The men in the
cave may be distinguished intellects but they would be ignorant
too, says Plato, because they are ruled by their sense-bound
rationalistic consciousness, whereas the true philosopher has
realized the truths the men in the cave are verbalizing about. This
basic distinction between the theorist and the existentialist in
philosophy is crucial in mysticism, and in Thoreau.

People said to him, Henry, you speak in riddles. His answer:
"You will pardon some obscurities, for there are more secrets in
my trade than in most men's."[13] His trade is the life of regeneration,
so there *will* be secrets from those not yet ready for the new life.

In these opening pages of his masterpiece we see the figure
of Thoreau beginning his Walden sojourn and establishing
groundwork for his momentum in the subsequent two years.
He's shown us the leitmotif in the negative sense—such as, what
I *don't* want—*their* way of living, *their* values. Now he will have
to introduce a more positive option, although the negative
element, as we have seen, does provide an energy of resistance.
Having done that, he is ready to *embrace* something as well as
to repudiate.

He tells us what kind of food he is eating: "It was fit that I
should live on rice, mainly, who loved so well the philosophy of
India." He becomes a vegetarian. Except for certain savage
moments of weakness that he cannot resist, frankly recorded in
the "Higher Laws" chapter. He told his mother that he didn't drink
coffee or tea anymore, not to speak of wine, and she was alarmed:
"I know a good woman who thinks that her son lost his life because
he took to drinking water only."

And yet there is an affectionate overtone for his mother in
this, who was not the easiest person to relate to. She was known as
the most talkative woman in Concord, but Thoreau always
maintained a filial respect for her and for her home cooking. His

father had nothing in common with him at any time. They would work together side by side in the elder's pencil shop, for hours, without speaking. There was no communication between them, yet Thoreau was careful to cultivate a dutiful respect for his father, as well. He related to them both as a spiritual seeker must, because of the parent's godlike role in our lives. The ungodly parent might be rejected or ignored, but are there many of these? Short of that, the potential mystic is asked to revere the parents because of their crucial function in his spiritual development. Thoreau knew this instinctively or may have read it in his precious religious books, but certainly embodied it, as Whitman did. A great man acts this way. It is the morally retarded man who repudiates his parents, fights with them, and scorns them. We may pass through that stage but it mustn't be permanent. We must get over it quickly.

Significantly, no one in Thoreau's or Whitman's families had any spiritual inclinations or development whatever. That is how it is in spiritual life. A genuine aspirant for self-transcendence never finds encouragement from his family. One can hardly think of a single case in Western history. In other words, such a negative attitude, according to this archetypal pattern, is almost necessary. Someone who seeks mystical experience or self-knowledge in a spiritual sense finds only opposition and discouragement from his family—at best indifference. It is almost invariably so.

The family is the nucleus of not only society but of Nature functioning *through* society. The family is Nature functioning in a societal way, bringing to bear upon the individual the force of the tribe, of blood, of flesh, of matter. He who is flesh of our flesh, bone of our bone, blood of our blood, wishes to become spirit, to become winged in our earthly midst—so we resist him. Consciously, of course, they do not think that way. Rather, it is an instinctive psychic awareness that one member of the clan is seeking other pastures, not merely to leave but to embrace another order of being that the family as such knows nothing about, as William Blake so bitterly laments in his poem, "To Tirzah."

The family is blind to spiritual reality. Individually they may have their moments of insight, they may pray, give alms, go to church, but as a family—as a unit, as a dynamic reality in itself, separate from the members that compose it, the family does not have a spiritual character. They exist as a tribal or naturalistic power that the potential aspirant must cope with every step of the way, sometimes has to leave, usually has to, and then may return to later, as Thoreau did.

Thoreau did the best he could with his parents, sisters, and relatives. During the years he was with them and writing his journals, while at the same time trying to love his father and mother, he was observing: "The household is the very haunt and lair of our vice"[14]— the gossip, suspicion, mutual recrimination, recalling Christ's statement that a man's enemies "shall be those of his own household."

By "man" he meant, as Thoreau means, the *questing* man, not the ordinary man who is comfortable with his family, as they are with him. He does not seek anything beyond their dimensions. The moment it is felt—and it will be felt instantly in a group tied together with such intimate tentacles of mutual awareness— that one member is seeking to become something they are not, they move in concert to defeat him. It is a universal rule and a secret of spiritual life that a man's foes shall be those of his own family.

The family is often glorified as a pillar of love and affection, which it is so long as one of their members is not seeking a reality beyond its ken. Then they can be mutually helpful, often warm hearths of comfort and repose, but the spiritual seeker lives in search of something else.

At one point during a gathering in Galilee, Christ was mingling with a number of people when his mother came to him and said, your brethren wait outside—that is, your brothers have come to see you about something. And he turned to her and said, who are my brethren, who are my sisters? All these here are my brothers and sisters—not just the ones that have come to see me. Everyone that does the will of God is my brother, they are all mine.

But the family doesn't understand. It represses this kind of awareness. Yet we must somehow be reconciled to them also because without the parents we would not have the wherewithal even to protest. To them we owe an irreplaceable debt that we can't begin to repay. The two realities confront us: the feeling that we can't communicate with them and at the same time can never be grateful enough. And the two have to be combined in one effort of spiritual reconciliation. Honor thy father and mother, says Christ, who, as noted, also said, a man's enemies shall be those of his own household.

You have to do both, you have to realize that the household cannot be of any help to you, cannot understand and are inimical to your true endeavors. But you are tied to them in so many ways that to renounce them is to renounce humanity. To reject them is to reject life. And we can't say, I accept humanity but not my family. So, if you want oneness with humanity and with life you have to start by being reconciled with the family. Meanwhile there is this block, this barrier—the difficulty of communication.

Thoreau worked at various jobs in the early years and succeeded best, perhaps, as a surveyor, although, as we know from *Walden,* he worked at this as little as necessary. The thing he was famous for in Concord was as leader of the huckleberry party. When the children went out on outings in the woods, he would be the one who went along with them. He knew the best places to go for huckleberries and the children gravitated to him. In discussing Thoreau's flawed personality we should also note that he loved children and they loved him. Emerson regretted this tendency. He said that with his gift for practical skill and executive action and insight, instead of engineering for all America, Thoreau was the captain of a huckleberry troop.

He didn't care for sophisticated people, while farmers and others living simply, close to the earth, attracted him. Birds and animals were part of his reality. He had a strange ease with them. They felt fearless in his presence. He would actually take them in his hand, creatures skittish in the presence of human beings. He could pull an animal out of a hole by its tail—something most of us would reluctantly attempt—without getting bitten. Birds, too, were drawn to him, would rest on his shoulder, sensing that he was not trying to hurt them. One recalls a similar phenomenon in the life of Francis of Assisi.

Unable to make up his mind what to do for a living, he determined to go to Walden Woods, raise a few beans and rice and live there, selling the beans to support himself. He didn't eat the beans because Pythagoras had declared they were not a spiritual food. This is the way he found his guru—in the mystical literature of the Orient and the ancient world. He lived on rice and fruit. "I also dreamed that I might gather wild herbs … but … trade curses everything it handles"[15]— reminding us of Buddha's Eightfold Path, which consists of the eight basic aspects of life that must be properly conceived, one of these being "right livelihood."

Any livelihood will not do for the spiritual aspirant. It has to be the right kind for his development as a potential mystic. One that will awaken egoism, selfishness, or similar moods would be inappropriate. Hence commerce and trade would not be acceptable because of the profit motive and its excitation of ego. In trade, in commerce, we are concerned primarily with making money, a motivation unworthy of a spiritual prospect. Whatever we do must not be driven by that element chiefly. If money is involved let it come as an afterthought. It shouldn't be involved directly in the work, which should absorb all our mind. If someone then pays us, well and good, but we must learn not to orient ourselves to that incentive. If we are in commerce of any kind whatever, this is impossible to do—we will always be thinking of the profit factor and hence our minds will be demeaned, debarring us from the contemplation of Truth. On the other hand, some occupations are in themselves spiritual and encourage the higher tendencies, seem to be intrinsically beneficial to the spiritual life.

The 1840s was an era of social reform in America. People said to him, Henry, you won't have a chance to do much good for your fellow man out there in the woods. His answer:

> While my townsmen and women are devoted in so
> many ways to the good of their fellows, I trust that one
> at least may be spared to other and less humane
> pursuits. You must have a genius for charity as well as
> for anything else. As for Doing-good, that is one of the
> professions which are full. Moreover, I have tried it
> fairly, and ... am satisfied that it does not agree with
> my constitution.

As before, his wit covers hidden meanings. It is not *doing* but *being* good that he wants. Those who don't understand the dynamics of this idea—of *being* as the prime requisite of life—will be reduced to doing good as the best they can achieve. But if the possibility of self-realization has dawned on us, then simply "doing-good" will exercise a more shadowy attraction. Thoreau again:

> If I were to preach at all in this strain, I should say
> rather, Set about being good. As if the sun should stop
> ... and go about like a Robin Goodfellow, peeping in at
> every cottage window ... instead of steadily increasing
> his genial heat ... till he is of such brightness that no
> mortal can look him in the face....

The sun fulfills itself by just being, in the blaze of its own radiance, recalling Blake's image of the sun and moon—if they paused for a moment to question their reality they would immediately vanish. Their objective is that of the brave man—being, and more being. Along the way they may do good, like a Buddha or a Christ, but do not set themselves out to *do* good as such, but rather to *become* something, to encompass a new reality, to experience a light of truth, and when this is achieved the whole world is benefited.

See how much the sun helps the world, he argued, not by attempting to do good but to continue in its being and to achieve more of the same. This is Thoreau's objective. It is what Christ meant when he said: "I came that men might have a greater abundance of life"—more sun-like self-awareness, more inner radiance. Then, doing good will be inevitable. The sun *must* do good by *being* good. A great soul must do good by being what he is. That is Thoreau's goal also: to achieve the *inner*—that is to say, the divine—goodness, and then everything he does will be a blessing to mankind. Again he distinguishes between the values of others and those of the mystic.

Everywhere we turn the mystic is traveling a different path. Alone at first, and Thoreau certainly was. He had for companions only the birds, the bees, and members of the animal kingdom. He never had much fellowship among men but perhaps it wasn't too necessary for him. In the end the loneliness ceases and the hour of mysticism—the hour of truth—brings us into an experience of the All. Then we feel united with everyone and instead of doing good, we achieve a goodness which permeates our awareness and is communicated by the sheer fact of existence. This All that we now possess is within, the new humanity we embrace is within. If it is an authentic experience the outer immediately responds to the inner, and there is a sense of cosmic oneness available to the illumined soul, for whom one touch of self-transcendence makes the whole world kin.

The Quest – Walden

Against this background of Thoreau's life and character we might profitably consider some of the highlights of *Walden*, but first there is the matter of Thoreau's long depression which still troubles a number of people.

As suggested earlier, in the case of the spiritual-striving man, depression is almost invariably caused by some nonalignment between insight and life. In other words, it is spiritually motivated. The ordinary man who doesn't have a desire to seek truth but merely goes where life directs him may have psychologically induced depression, as we all might to some degree. But the momentous turn that takes place in our destiny when we begin to seek the inner man, the ultimate truth, is of radical significance in comparison to the life that most people live. There is frequently a reversal of values. Hence the depressions of a person geared to the senses and to worldly ideals may be solved by psychological methods but the spiritual man's depressions are unique. He has introduced himself to a whole different set of possibilities when he becomes a spiritual prospect and as a result has many more reasons to become depressed than the ordinary man.

Depression literally means a "pressing-down," a sinking-down, a receding. In our spiritual life we have times of growth, of progress, of strength and enthusiasm, and then we have periods of an opposite nature, the intervals of depression. Sometimes they are called dryness, and when the dry period becomes particularly heavy, we call it depression.

As noted previously, one of the spiritual directors of India said not allowing your mind to get into depression was the chief problem in spiritual life. Even if we have an ideal personality for the path and an auspicious background that might relieve us of many psychological complications to disturb our equanimity— depressions cannot be avoided. Christ and Buddha themselves knew of depressions.

This is the nature of the path: to have cycles of depression; along with them, periods of great energy. No one can escape the phenomenon. The only thing we can do is to live with it and to realize when it comes. It is like other physiological periods that beset men and women. They don't always like it but they get used to it. Depression is that, periodic, unavoidable. It is proof that we are struggling to become new beings when we have these oscillations of spirit.

Ultimately any depression can be seen essentially in this light, even among worldly people. For these individuals as well are made in the image and likeness of the divine, and though they are moving in a fog of many-layered ignorance, at bottom they have the awareness of spiritual realities. When we encounter one of them, how suddenly attuned they are to the difference between our way of life and theirs.

In short, in everyone's case depression can be spiritually oriented. Certainly it is true in the case of the actively spiritual man who may have no real problem of personality. This was Thoreau's case.

He had reached an authentic height at Walden, tried to maintain it for seven years afterwards while writing the book, creatively reliving his heroic period, that two-year dramatic gesture that has captured the imagination of so many: that perfect time at Walden. Then he seems to sink slowly, cannot maintain his pitch, and the years bring depression in 1855, lasting more than a year. He cannot shake it off. No one has explained it, but it is in fact no mystery: he was unable to generate further willpower in himself to create another Walden, to raise himself to an equal or higher pitch. He lacked the psychic energy of this challenge and didn't know how to go about doing it. For one thing, there was the necessity of spiritual association, the role of some tradition of mysticism. Here is Henry Thoreau, the hero trying to do it all alone, outside of a tradition, trying to forge his own.

The Transcendental framework provided a kind of tradition in his age. It was in fact, as we have noted, an intellectual conversation-piece, as far as any reality emerging from it is concerned. They merely wrote and talked about metaphysical things. They wanted to bring about many changes, but not to themselves.

Many of us face Thoreau's dilemma even today, in that we have broken away from various faiths, backgrounds, and orthodoxies and are seeking truth. At the very least we need guidance, spiritual association. We cannot do it on our own. Look at Thoreau—and he a rare individual. We can't assume we have his strength to begin with, as we know he had it in such abundance. If he had had a guide, or spiritual companionship, people doing the same thing as he, seeking what he was, namely, divine reality, seeking to know it directly, to see it and to become one with it—if he had known someone like that he might have received mysterious guidance that occurs when, as Christ says, two or three are gathered together in his name—he is there. By Christ, we mean the *divine* is there.

Whenever two or three are brought together earnestly seeking enlightenment, they will find guidance even though they are individually not qualified to be gurus—they'll be lights to each other. Compensation will be made. Ideally we might have a teacher or a guide, someone who has been where we have not yet been, who has climbed the mountain to a certain point where we have not yet gone, and tells us, "At this level you have these experiences, difficulties, moods, dangers. I encountered them and heard that others encountered them too." And then the aspirant comes, reaches that point, says, "You're right, it's as you say." They experience the same things—zones of consciousness everyone passes through—whether we're on the path of Zen, the Christian path or the Vedantic path, it doesn't matter.

These disciplines, paths, orientations are essentially temperamental in origin. We choose one which, as from a smorgasbord buffet, is the kind of food we like. Which doesn't mean that we will escape any of the classic battles in the life of regeneration. We choose Zen, Vedanta, Christianity, or Sufism depending on something in them that temperamentally appeals to us, and that, not its intrinsic truth, is the justification for accepting it.

They all are inspired. All have drawbacks. All have ignorance enmeshed in them. But each has proven strength to regenerate. The ideal is to attach ourselves to one of these and to say, this is for me. Which doesn't mean it is universally the best, any more than the food we choose is for everyone.

The discipline is something we embrace because it appeals to us, but the psychological patterns of the new life are predictable, and one of its intrinsic parts is depression, or dryness. At some point we begin to look for causes outside of ourselves. But the world within has causes enough—a vast universe. And therein lies the source of our depressions.

The prolonged existence of ego produces the depression. We don't find depressions in the lives of saints who, as St. Catherine of Siena said, "have passed over the thorn." There are none, in short, in the lives of realized souls. All such things are behind them. Depressions are a part of the landscape of growth; we don't experience them on the top of the mountain.

After we have made some progress we feel ourselves growing spiritual and strong—and *real*. But the ego's tendrils are deeply entwined in us, which is another thing to live with, the discovery that we have with us the adversary, its roots clutched into the psyche and around the soul, as it were, in a fast embrace. One by one we loosen the tentacles of this cage, the spectre-grip upon us. Every act of service, of unselfishness, loosens one more tentacle, but there are hundreds remaining. We have been a long time creating them, not only in the present lifetime but in many, many others, which would explain the existence of this mysterious power. One life—it is difficult to imagine how we could become so egocentric in just twenty or thirty years. It seems inconceivable that we would have *such* difficulty made by our own hands in such a short time. Hence, the thought that many lifetimes have contributed.

But after these periods of advance, what depresses us is the sudden realization that we are our old selves again: *that* is the depression, that is the cause of it. Thoreau discovered this life after Walden, after writing about it. Perhaps spending too much time writing about it, failing to emerge in a fresh light, creating another Walden, a new adventure. He was doing what all of us like to do, rehearsing our great moments over and over. For seven years he did this, repeating himself constantly in the rewriting of the book, giving us the masterpiece—but literature does not provide spiritual progress.

At the end of that time he discovered he was the same self he had always been.

To speak truly, it was an admirable self. He was undoubtedly the greatest of his contemporaries, but in his own eyes his few flaws were egregious blemishes. For a really holy person, to discover any of the shreds of the old self will be demoralizing, whereas most of us live with a mountain of faults and think we are good examples to others.

So Thoreau, now as before, found himself arrogant, resentful, indignant at his fellows. That may have been the cause. Still struggling with the lower nature as he recorded in "Higher Laws," unable to become free of the creature-man. It could have been these, or other reasons, to make him feel his advance was blocked. And so he continued, on the momentum of the past, as we also are inclined to do. He had no one to help him generate a breakthrough experience. The ego returned in all its fury, not as it had been, but fiery and tormenting. That alone would cause depression.

Then, along with the resurgence of ego, his book, his masterpiece, is received casually by his contemporaries. Had he been egoless, he wouldn't have spent seven years on the book—he would have created other books, other *Waldens*. That he spent so much time rewriting it means that he was still egocentric. We understand his motivation and from our standpoint we're glad he did it—but not from his own.

Wasn't it escapism for Thoreau at Walden? As his peers said, Henry, you're not going to help mankind out there. Thoreau disagreed. It is like a man on a burning ship, aware of the ship being destroyed. His companions do not realize the flames are enveloping them. The ship is on fire! he cries out, let's get off! And they reply, where are the flames? *He* is aware of them, as John Bunyon was at the beginning of *Pilgrim's Progress,* with his allegorical hero Christian in the chapter called "The City of Destruction." In that work Christian wakes up as from a dream and suddenly sees the city of destruction all around him like Thoreau in Concord in the America of the 1840s: The world is in flames, and I want to get away from it. Christian cries: "What shall I do? How shall I live?" This is Thoreau's cry at Walden. The cry of all of us. We awake to the fact that we live in the city of destruction. What shall we do? How shall we live our lives? It is like a houseboat slowly sinking and everyone says, the water is the same as it has always been. We however see that the boat is really sinking. We want to go to the shore. Finally we leave them after urging them to go with us. They say, "No, that's escapism. Stay with us." And the boat goes down.

So Thoreau felt about the city of the nineteenth century as we might feel about the city of this century. He wanted to escape from the world of the cave. The men in Plato's cave would have said to someone who got up from his hunched ignorance, "That's not the light. You're running away from everything you hold dear. You are escaping." But it isn't escapism. It is realism. It is the discovery of the life that people call real is unreal. We are seeking another city, another reality. Of course we do have to go through that period of resistance and struggle with others, who will call us hard names sometimes, may use words like escapism. Thoreau, we know, was attacked with this criticism and he gives a very strong answer to it.

We could study almost every page in a semi-scripture like *Walden*—any work written by an illumined soul being scriptural to one degree or another. Scriptures are the symbolic fruits of the realizations of saints and sages and may occur at any time. Thoreau at least was on that path, hence *Walden* and its religious tone. It doesn't speak in religious terms as such but there is a sublime aura about the book. Two selections from his early journals, which were mentioned previously reinforce this idea. As early as 1841 when he was only twenty-four he was already pining for the transcendental life that he could realize at Walden. The excerpts were written eight months apart:

> I only ask a clean seat. I will build my lodge on the southern slope of some hill, and take there the life the gods send me. Will it not be employment enough to accept gratefully all that is yielded me between sun and sun?...[1]

> I want to go soon and live away by the pond, where I shall hear only the wind whispering among the reeds. It will be success if I shall have left myself behind.[2]

The first of these is written on the Monday of Easter week and the second, two days before Christmas the same year. So, although Thoreau was not a churched Christian, two famous religious periods in the Christian year evoked in him religious sentiments which he identified with Walden. Going there becomes an act of piety, self-purification. He becomes a pilgrim to himself— to his unknown self.

The self to be left behind is the self of the City of Destruction. It isn't only others who are destroying themselves, we are also—we have the same self that is destroying them. It is the self that destroys, not the "world." The City of Destruction is within, not without. Pollution of the environment is only a phase of our degeneration—a symptom of what ails us psychologically. Which doesn't mean that we shouldn't put our hand to that, solving that problem too. If we wait until everyone is regenerated before examining the environment we might all be living in the slums. It is good that some people, appropriately motivated, will accept that challenge, and good that others, not so motivated, like Thoreau, would do the other work. Between them we can perfect the work of grace.

To repeat: the true destroyer is the self within. The City of Destruction, that Christian feared, was inward.

The whole pilgrimage is an allegory of many places, all of which are within. Which is what an allegory does—delineates, sometimes in widely spaced physical terms the phenomenology of the internal life. Plato's Cave—the life of shadows, the life of the fire, the life of the sun, the escape from the one, the escape to the other—all within. Allegory merely symbolizes what is taking place on the internal stage.

Thoreau said that doing good didn't agree with his constitution and that he would have to try something else: to *be* good—doing good is difficult to achieve unless you know who you are. If we do good with the ordinary self we expect some recognition from our good work. This is the taint of egoism, which gets into everything. We expect, if not exactly reward, some appreciation for our efforts. Everyone does this. It is unenlightened living nevertheless. Thoreau's strong analogy to the sun comes to mind here; the sun doesn't look into windows trying to do good with its light and warmth, but simply dwells high in the empyrean of its own consciousness and its light and warmth fill the world. This is what we should do. Then every act, every impulse, will be good, we won't anticipate anything else. If we already have it we won't expect applause as well.

"Rescue the drowning and tie your shoestrings"[3]—that should be our response. Don't let the left hand know what the right hand does; don't let the ego say, what a great thing I've done. Act as though you weren't acting. This is the approach of Zen. Every religion has food for all of us, even though we are not on that particular path. In Zen it is—the light touch. Do great things—lightly, as though not doing them. "Rescue the drowning and tie your shoestrings."

Hence the depth in the old saying: Virtue is its own reward—good actions make us spiritual and unselfish. What could be better? But we have to undertake them in the right spirit. If we do not, we expect recompense or recognition. If we see them as an act of spiritual discipline, an offering to our own newly emerging selves, we won't look for anything beyond that knowledge. *Be* good, that is, become spiritual and then everything you do will be good—what Thoreau attempted to do. It was *his* escapism. You might remember that when people say what you are doing is escapism, we are not escaping *from* something but *into* something: a new personality. Having done so, we will then return to the others who are yet bound in their cave-consciousness and may be able to attract them out of it.

This is what Thoreau was seeking. Is his way the best way? Perhaps not any more. His world was still almost medieval in its quietness. He found Concord with its two thousand inhabitants rather too large for his taste, for he was a born monastic. Nevertheless we need a scripture for our age. All the scriptures have been written by monks; we need one written for householders, as most of us are now. Thoreau's is not quite adequate. *Walden* is semi-scriptural. He would be someone to write a scripture had he gone a little further than he did and overcome the arrogance, scorn, indignation and aloofness that flawed him to the end. He would have to get free from all that.

Would a new scripture invalidate the old? Of course not. The principles of scriptures deal with the very essence of consciousness, with absolute elements which change not. Likewise, the truths of the world's authentic scriptures can never change. We could, if we wished, find the common core of those truths by comparing the five or six major religions. Those aspects wherein they sharply differ from one another we could discard as not being universal enough for our consideration. We could still find a good deal that is essential in all of them and declare that *this* is the truth of life. Interpretations and attitudes would vary because temperaments vary, but nevertheless they would be an impressive body of objective findings. These will always be the same. They are the most precious of all writings. In fact, they are the only writings. Everything else appeals to us to give us a kind of satisfaction or entertainment—or stimulus of some kind. But either directly or indirectly, all the other great books are great—like *Walden*—insofar as they resemble the scriptures in their insights.

How can we feel comfortable with these traditional scriptures? We often feel that they are meant for another generation. Yet we can't deny the truths that are there, the laws that are expounded. What's the answer, then? A different approach is needed to reach the unchanging truth than the monastic. Earlier we asked if Thoreau's way is appropriate for us. Perhaps not, except for relatively few truly geared to live his kind of life. We always need some who will go and live the ascetic life and come back and tell us how it is—as *Walden* does.

But it is hard to renounce contact with our contemporaries the way Thoreau so triumphantly did and the way monastics so effortlessly do. We are finding this difficult to do more and more, as though we have a duty not only to seek our own salvation but to emancipate each other. There is little of this in Thoreau.

Not that what he gives us isn't precious and valuable. No one saint can give us everything, not even a divine incarnation. Christ doesn't answer all of our sentiments, or needs. There are times when we feel more like attaching ourselves to Buddha, in the Buddha-mood and vice versa. The Buddhist cannot be satisfied with Buddha alone after he discovers Christ—his love, humility, devotional, sacrificial nature. Buddha expressed these virtues in a different way. But Christ's is another experience entirely. The Buddhist says, what a wonderful life, I want to be like that. Just these two, and still between them they don't exhaust all our possibilities. We are grateful for what Thoreau gives us but we would like something more.

In other words, the traditional approach to eternal truths is to be modified. Monastic renunciation and seclusion is not the way any more. A contemporary scripture could enlighten our path about this. People like Blake, Whitman, Thoreau, Gibran, Tagore, Vivekananda, and others are, as it were, creating modern sacred texts between them. No one towers enough above the others to constitute a scripture in itself, but each is making a strong contribution.

There are others we could name. Gandhi is one. We have his autobiography with its arresting subtitle: *My Experiments with Truth*. What is truth? he asked. If truth is real let it instruct us at each step of the way. This idea was his path. I would assume nothing, all I know is there is a truth, I feel it, I've been told it is real, I accept the integrity of the sages who have declared it does exist, but I don't know exactly what it is. I must know it myself. Let all my actions, thoughts, words and attitudes be brought to the bar of judgment: what is the truth trying to be revealed to me in this action, conversation, relationship, attitude, plan? For Gandhi it was an experiment. He made many errors which he admitted, but the path he was on enabled him to find out what was *not* in error. So darkness helped light reveal itself—a phenomenon that would be a significant contribution to a new scripture.

The relations between men and women are a big part of it. This whole area has to be reevaluated. The old way—Thoreau's way—is not adequate. Instead of renouncing or sublimating each other, we must perfect each other *in* the relationship. We must find a way to do it.

Man, instead of renouncing woman because of her beauty, must worship her because of it, which is a special manifestation of the divine in human life ... especially that inner beauty which is hers as well, and which will advance his progress to final illumination, if he knows how to relate to it rather than fleeing from it.

Worship, mutual devotion, a sharing oneness of spirit, a union of eternal principles—this way will be one of the themes of the scripture to come.

In *Walden* we read: "There are a thousand hacking at the branches of evil to one who is striking at the root."[4]

The branches of evil are a thousandfold, there is no end to them. While others are telling him to do good works, Thoreau wants to strike at the root. Good works tackle the branches, hack them down: poverty, sickness, overpopulation, disease. These are worthy objectives, but where is their root? Thoreau finds the root in himself: the ignorance within, the ego, the spectre, the separate self that wants to live as a law unto itself. This is the root. St. Paul said that the love of money was the root of all evil, but Thoreau would argue there was something still deeper—love of money being simply one of its branches.

To strike at this root you need discipline and solitude. In modifying the scriptural injunctions of the past you must not forget the lessons they have to teach us. They affirm the necessity of solitude and silence, which we have to have. It is hard if we are raising a family or living with other people with whom we have to associate. Many of us have known this classic modern difficulty. The spiritual aspirant of today has to face problems unknown to monastic seekers of the past.

Compensation will be made. We are assured of this. We don't have quite the same strength that people used to have. What are we going to do then? Will we be lost because somehow in the last few hundred years we have let ourselves go astray and now that it is very late we are trying to get back to the path but are struggling with weakened minds and personalities?

Compensation will be necessary. Most of us do not have Thoreau's strength to truly renounce as he did, to simply turn around and leave our contemporaries alone, thinking, let them destroy themselves. And if we did, is that the way? Some of us may have the strength but may not be motivated to act in that manner.

In any case we are bound up by the new century, which is nonspiritual in its essential direction. Yet simultaneously a spiritual current has appeared as a saving antidote, so that in the world looming some will get through. The torch of truth and mysticism will be carried on by a few people who will not be lost, whatever darkness lies ahead of us. We need many spiritual aspirants for that, so that there is a vanguard of seekers to keep alive the priceless heritage—the only one that mankind has. All the others sooner or later erode and are replaced by something else. All the great empires have had this happen to them, but the mystical heritage remains— the one that can save man eventually and which must be kept alive. Therefore we need hundreds of thousands of seekers so that at least a portion—a few thousand—will be available for the future of the race, and of the world.

These are with us as a universal compensation for the main tendency in our time which is not spiritual. We've been caught up in the current of egoism and have been degenerated and victimized by it. Allowance must be made for us. If any of you were the super-intending deity of the universe you would certainly make allowance. Or, to impersonalize it, the divine intelligence itself, aware of differences between generations and centuries, would do so.

Everything is not inflexibly the same from one century to another. We have been reassured of that by modern mystics. We don't have to do the same things that men used to do to achieve liberation. Things are difficult now for the spiritual seeker; we don't have the inducement to avail ourselves of monastic sources of strength, as householders once did. Even if we have the stamina for monasticism we are discouraged from it by a feeling of loyalty to our fellows.

Yet we have to have some discipline, some solitude, and if we can't get it in the fields, we will find it in our own house. Two periods every day devoted to solitude and silence is necessary. We bring our monastery into our own home. If we can't find it outside anymore, if our Waldens are no longer in existence, then we have to create an equivalent reality within the house at least once a day; have to give the mind a taste of its own essence, of what it really is, and not a taste of everything else, which in full ignorance it is running after.

This is the practice of meditation, concentration, and other spiritual disciplines whereby the imprisoned splendor of the mind can be tapped and gradually reflected upon the screen of consciousness. It can't be done without systematic silence and solitude. This is one of the indispensable truths we learn from scriptures and there can be no compromise about it, as there can be none about the end in sight. But we do modify the means somewhat. Also we need spiritual association—all the scriptures emphasize this. They often use the phrase "the company of the holy." Such individuals will enhance and strengthen in us the virtues we want to awaken, guide us if we don't have a guru, and form an existential background if we are proceeding outside of a tradition. Thoreau availed himself of none of this. It is a wonder he went as far as he did.

People said he was self-centered. His reply: "I never dreamed of any enormity greater than I have committed. I never knew, and never shall know, a worse man than myself." The ego, the spectre, which he went to Walden to remove is the enormity within, the criminal inmate of our secret minds. "I believe that what so saddens the reformer ... is his private ail."[5] Again—as within, so without.

The problem of conquest is self-conquest. Alexander, who had mastered the known world at the age of thirty-three, made the mistake of thinking that the world to be conquered was out there. Everything that could be conquered, was. He had nothing left but drunkenness and sensuality, and died in an alcoholic rout one night. An unforgettable example of the impermanence of outer dominion. If he had put that willpower to work on the inner world we might have had another Zoroaster or a Buddha. The strength is the same in each case. As far down as you have gone into weakness and degeneracy, you can go as high in virtue and self-realization.

Most of our fellows are neither saints nor sinners. It presumes a powerful determination and self-confidence to settle on a way of life that flouts the mores of others. We know how potent public opinion is in its effect on all of us. To repudiate this, to become a renegade, is an act of strength, among other things. Hitler was certainly a strong personality. He drew so many into his orbit by his magnetic power. It was simply misdirected. Such people will have to undo all they have done. They will have to start a long way back but the driving force that demonizes them will make them eventually into saints.

Gandhi had the same strength as Hitler. He also attracted millions into his orbit. He had a magnetic personality, people could not resist it, they went everywhere, did everything he said—it was the same phenomenon as with Hitler. One living as a name of infamy, the other as a name of holiness: power behind both of them—the tremendous force of the human will, the human personality. God-like. Alexander the Great will someday turn the power that conquered worlds into the vaster world within.

The drunkard is a potential saint. He is seeking a consciousness that will give him peace and fulfillment, as sense-consciousness fails to do. He is seeking a super-sensual awareness and seems to achieve it in alcohol. The drug addict also. But the drive that motivates them is the same drive that motivates the saint, that motivated Thoreau. I am not satisfied, they say, with this sense-consciousness, this ordinary nonmystical, ego-centered mindset. I want something else.

What he wants is not out there. That too is within: innumerable states of mind within. The alcoholic or the drug addict unfortunately mistakes the means and ends disastrously—will have to undo all the bad karma. We sympathize with their motivation and know what is propelling them, namely—the urge to mystical experience. This is the main force behind alcoholism and drug addiction, bringing us back to that earlier statement about depression. Perhaps all depression is ultimately spiritual if we look at it deeply enough.

So we have the alcoholic defiantly and desperately challenging his contemporaries—I don't like your way of life, I want something else. The best he can do is reach for alcohol or drugs. The sensualist, too—Don Juan, the same thing. He is not satisfied with ordinary life, wants an absolute experience. The alcoholic wants that moment of glory, which he thinks will change his personality forever—if he could only find it. Then when he comes back from the experience he'll be happy and everything will be all right. This is pitiful motivation. The alcoholic, the drug addict, the sensualist—the extreme man. All driven in the same way. We sympathize with them knowing what their motivation is, they are souls too, and the soul is really always functioning.

Hitler, too. He really thought he would help the world, help Germany. Behind all the evil, the demonism, he was a soul, and as much as Gandhi, thought he would save his country, save Germany from her enemies.

Yet the alcoholic and the drug addict will have to undo all the negativism somehow. As Buddha said, there is no power in the three worlds that can preserve a man from the result of his actions; therefore, he added, do good actions.

"Renew thyself completely each day," writes Thoreau. "Morning," he says, "brings back the heroic ages." As the afternoon weakens us and the evening depresses us, sometimes we feel another day is lost, but each morning recreates a sense of the heroic: "After a partial cessation of a sensuous life, the soul of man, or its organs rather, are reinvigorated each day, its Genius tries again what noble life it can make."[6]

Notice the subtle distinction in the line, "the soul of man, or its organs rather." The soul of man never sleeps but its organs sleep, the body sleeps, the mind sleeps. The instruments of the soul, ministers of the king, exclaim, Wake up, wake up! I have things to do, and the mind is sluggish, the body likewise, the senses are confused; and of course the ego is always there in the background trying to disorganize everything, while the soul constantly attempts to command this sluggish host to do its transcendental bidding.

"The millions are awake enough for physical labor; but only one in a million … for effective intellectual exertion, only one in a hundred million to the poetic or divine life." Here poetic means *prophetic* as William Blake used it, or *mystical*. Only one in a hundred million, recalling Krishna's similar statement in the *Bhagavad Gita:* "One in a thousand seeks me…" Just *one*, at first lacking the strength of self-realization, feeling somewhat inadequate and uncertain, instinctively seeks out congenial aspirants wherever he can find them. Monks always gather together for this reason. One from each town. In each of their communities they were isolated, singled out as strange, potential neurotics. We become neurotic when we are unable to maintain the balance of stress between our own drives and the social pressures on us. Until we get the strength of self-knowledge we often yield to this conflict. One solution is to find even one other person who thinks the way we do. We meet together, then another joins us, soon we've got a commune.

"To be awake is to be alive. I have never yet met a man who was quite awake. How could I have looked him in the face?" This theme is all through his journals. Now and then, at long intervals, you meet a really holy person or a saint, and you see that they don't look like other people, their eyes, their faces are unlike others'.

Buddha was one day sitting under a tree when a man came up to him, stared and asked: Are you a god? Buddha said, no. Are you a man? Buddha said, no. Are you a celestial? No. What are you? Buddha replied, I am the awakened—I am awake. I am what it is to be awake. The man had not asked, *who* are you, but *what* are you—the same question that is always directed to great prophets, Christ for one, as well as St. Francis. If you really meet an awakened man it does not occur to you to ask, who are you, as you might with ordinary men. You say, what is this? In his journals Thoreau often expressed the view that he would go anywhere to meet a man who is awake, if he could only find one.

We see that this yearning for guidance was there. He had a hunger for direction; he knew that he couldn't do it alone. None of us can.

> We must learn to reawaken and keep ourselves awake, not by mechanical aids, but by an infinite expectation of the dawn, which does not forsake us in our soundest sleep. I know of no more encouraging fact than the unquestionable ability of man to elevate his life by a conscious endeavor.

The Transcendentalists, artists, and intellectuals in all ages have tended to concentrate their genius for spirituality on outward things—books, music, paintings, philosophies, science—which is acceptable for a stage that we go through, but is only a stage. It is still outward. So Thoreau says:

> It is something to be able to paint a particular picture, or to carve a statue, and so to make a few objects beautiful; but it is far more glorious to carve and paint the very atmosphere and medium through which we look, which morally we can do. To affect the quality of the day, that is the highest of arts. Every man is tasked to make his life, even in its details, worthy of the contemplation of his most elevated and critical hour.

This is what he tried to do. We feel the truth of the man in the sentence he wrote, and when we look further at his life we are corroborated. Part of the aura of *Walden* is the sense it conveys that here is a man who really tried to live these high truths.

People kept asking him: "Why did you go to the woods?"

> I went to the woods because I wished to live deliber-
> ately, to front only the essential facts of life [the inward
> facts] and see if I could not learn what it had to teach,
> and not, when I came to die, discover that I had not
> lived. I did not wish to live what was not life, living is
> so dear.

In view of this he will condemn newspapers for reasons obvious to us now. They only strengthen a part of him that he wanted to attenuate and besides, he said, if you've read one newspaper, you've read them all. The principle behind them is merely repeated in each edition.

> Men esteem truth remote.... But ... God himself
> culminates in the present moment, and will never be
> more divine in the lapse of all the ages.

Why should God be found anywhere else but here? Why should the center of the universe be anywhere but in yourself? Why shouldn't it be where *you* are? This would also be the center of the godhead, since the godhead is not an anthropomorphic deity located in one place in time, it is pure spirit, pure being— why would the center of that be any one place in particular? God, says Christ, is a spirit to be worshiped in truth and in spirit. The center of that spirit could be with you as much as anywhere, and it is mysticism which discovers this.

Mysticism unveils this grandest of truths, which we're hearing more and more about in the present day. The center of things is not to be found outside of us, but within. We cannot hear this too often. We hear it, read it, meditate on it, and then go on and act as if we haven't heard it at all. We have to continually reinforce this idea of meditation and reading over and over again until it becomes part of our very being. Hearing about it once will not do. We have to hear about it for years.

He sits sometimes on the front step of his little cabin after he had breakfast and the sun has just risen—sits there for hours and sometimes when he looks up it is noon, or afternoon, the whole time in a reverie—profound meditation, one might think.

There is a difference between the two. Meditation means effort, concentration of the total mind. What Thoreau has experienced is reverie—passive, beautiful, enchanting, but not true meditation. Had he known this secret it would have saved him from a depression that lasted not a few days, or perhaps even a week or two, which we normally can't escape, but more than a year—which we can certainly escape. He didn't know about the art of meditation, spiritual disciplines. No one told him, least of all Emerson, who didn't meditate to begin with. In all the literature of the Transcendentalists there are no references to this theme.

There was no encouragement for this kind of interior knowing. It was all Nature, intellect, a cultivation of high moods but not a mapping and exploration of the internal world, nothing about concentration.

Thoreau never found this out. He had encountered the word *meditation,* the reference, in book after book in his Oriental readings, but assumed that perhaps *this*—this reverie, for instance—was meditation. Wordsworth assumed that meditation consisted of serene reflections in an idyllic spot in England's lake district where nature seems in a state of repose, and one falls into that state too, and then writes a poem about it, thinking *that* will be meditation.

There's a place for reverie, the passive aspect of meditation. We can't always be active, always seeking, we have to wait, be receptive, but this is not the main thing. It is a negative part of the action, in the sense of being the other part of the alternating rhythm.

Thoreau never discovered this—one of his greatest tragedies. With his spiritually rich nature, it wasn't pointed out to him. So the best he could do was to read, which doesn't go deep enough, merely stimulates us. Or sit in those reveries in the sunshine, which gives us a transient feeling of intuitive knowledge, of peace. Or he would take his long walks in the woods for four or five hours at a time, a substitute for yoga exercises and meditation. He called it his holy time, didn't want any one with him, both at Walden and in the years following.

Even when he returned to his mother's house after Walden, he was able every day to go to the woods. He simply slept at home, worked with his father, but managed four or five hours a day in the woods, trying in this cumbersome manner to gradually elevate his mind to a level of spiritual consciousness where it could be maintained—the same thing we attempt to do in meditation. He would walk relaxed. When his body was in pain he found he could actually relax it by walking. It was a disciplined walking, it was not a *sauntering*. It was his yoga.

The external world with its variety, its flora and fauna, became a tangible symbol of the inner world. But he should have done his walking within and not without. He wouldn't have had to consume four or five hours at a time to attain an integration and clarity which a half hour of meditation would have better achieved.

The Divine waits. We have to find the way. Here is Thoreau with all his spirituality, failing. He goes far but could have become a saint within his lifetime and would have illumined the whole century, with his great literary gift.

> There were times when I could not afford to sacrifice
> the bloom of the present moment to any work,
> whether of the head or hands....[7]

This is like a fruit of his austerity, these beautiful moments of trance and reverie, which however do not penetrate into the eternal world. It is nature-given. It is sense-born. The sun, the silence, the sounds of the time, all he does is allow himself to be possessed by the surroundings. To varying degrees we've all had this type of sublime experience. Wordsworth, as much as any man ever did, had them but they failed to touch his character. The struggle, the discipline, was missing.

Thoreau is famous for his interpretation of nature and her creatures. She gives him the innocence and simplicity that men do not, so he turns to her as to an attentive mother and embraces her. She gives him silence and solitude, the elements in which he seems to find himself.

Then the animals of nature, strange animals—owls for instance. But Thoreau "rejoices that there are owls." Blake's Doctrine of Correspondences is shared by all mystics—some more explicitly than others. That is, there is a correspondence between the inner and outer realms, everything that exists in the world around us has its inner reality in man. If we go deep enough into ourselves we can relate—symbolically, spiritually—to everything that exists. Not only animate but inanimate things, trees, plants, stones, hills, precious gems, colors—everything has an internal analogue.

> I rejoice that there are owls. Let them do the idiotic
> and maniacal hooting for men. It is a sound admirably
> suited to swamps and twilight woods which no day
> illustrates, suggesting a vast and undeveloped nature
> which men have not recognized. They represent the
> stark twilight and unsatisfied thoughts which all have.[8]

Or baby partridges. He looks into their eyes. What does he find that has a correspondence with something within him?

> The remarkably adult yet innocent expression of their
> open and serene eyes is very memorable. All intelli-
> gence seems reflected in them. They suggest not merely
> the purity of infancy, but a wisdom clarified by
> experience. Such an eye was not born when the bird
> was, but is coeval with the sky it reflects.[9]

As though they are vessels of some mysterious intelligence working in them as it works in sages. And in foxes:

> Sometimes I heard the foxes as they ranged over the
> snowcrust, in moonlight nights, in search of a
> partridge or other game, barking raggedly and
> demonically like forest dogs, as if laboring with some
> anxiety, or seeking expression, struggling for light and
> to be dogs outright and run freely in the streets; for if
> we take the ages into account, may there not be a
> civilization going on among brutes as well as men?
> They seemed to me to be rudimental, burrowing men,
> still standing on their defence, awaiting their
> transformation....[10]

The idea of awakening pervades his work—awakening *himself:* the Buddhist approach, which affirms the possibility of man accomplishing his own rebirth.

> Any prospect of awakening or coming to life to a dead
> man makes indifferent all times and places. The place
> where that may occur is always the same, and
> indescribably pleasant to all our senses.... Nearest to
> all things is that power which fashions their being.[11]

This is what Blake would say also, perceiving a world in a grain of sand and a heaven in a wild flower. Zen would declare: if you look at anything closely enough you will see the meaning for its existence. You will see the truth that it is in the universe to embody, however humble, and you will find the joy in that realization, so that anything can become, in Keats's phrase, a thing of beauty and a joy forever.

> *Next* to us the grandest laws are continually being
> executed. *Next* to us is not the workman whom we
> have hired ... but the workman whose work we are.

That would be the soul, the workman that has created us, that is shaping us into a fit agent from its divine potentialities. We are the workman of ourselves.

"However intense my experience, I am conscious of the presence and criticism of a part of me ... that is no more I than it is you." Along with his nature-given personality, the one that he went to Walden to leave behind, he discovers another self within him, a spectator, a divine witness for all his actions.

Periodically we have the feeling that someone is watching us— the soul-power, the soul-mind in us passing judgment on our imperfections. *And it is no more I than it is you.* In other words, what in me is the witness is the same in you which is the witness, and both are one. That, we might say, is God he is talking about. Perhaps it is his version of the Upanishadic truth that the soul of man is a part of the universal Soul. It does not belong to the individual.

Then what is this phenomenal self doing all the works? That is the separate, limited and mortal element of our being. That which is watching over it is an immortal witness—and is the same for every man.

The multiplicity of forms we see is a kind of mirage, an *appearance* of reality—not a true reality, like seeing a snake in the darkness, then discovering it was a rope after all. So the reality of bodies and human encounters seems to be real, each form seems to be separate, but the true reality is that which we have in common. It is no more I than it is you.

But after the first flush of enthusiasm in his twenties he has discovered that the road to *realization* is long and arduous. Vigilance is a virtue not to be overestimated:

> "That in which men differ from brute beasts," [quoting the sage Mencius], "is a thing very inconsiderable. The common herd lose it very soon; superior men preserve it carefully." Who knows what sort of life would result if we had attained to purity? If I knew so wise a man as could teach me purity I would go seek him forthwith.[12]

This is the mystic, the pure man. He has touched purity and then knows what impurity is. He doesn't call it evil. He would call it an obstacle to the purity. Thoreau exclaims: how can I get out of this impurity that binds me? Again his cry for guidance. And our cry.

Thoreau is a vegetarian but sometimes has a sudden hunger for fish and flesh which he gives into, like a bestial attack: "I felt the strange thrill of savage delight, and was strongly tempted to seize and devour him [a woodchuck] raw; not that I was hungry then, except for that wildness which he represented." In other words, Thoreau is in the process of not only giving up meat, but savagery. Wildness is the real thing he wants to give up. However, it isn't easily quelled, and the woodchuck represents the part of him that would still like to live on. In reaching the woodchuck he is reaching back into what he has been. *Not that I was hungry then.*

The savage desire, then, was not so much for food but for the *animal consciousness* which he, like all of us, has to work with:

Once or twice ... while I lived at the Pond, I found myself ranging the woods, like a half-starved hound, with a strange abandonment, seeking some kind of venison which I might devour and no morsel could have been too savage for me.

This is Thoreau, who quested for the holy life. This is what we have to contend with, this is part of our being, and the way lies *through* this dimension. But if we can recognize it, we can live with it. We can say, that's all right, it is the animal in me again coming forth. Tomorrow morning I start anew. I'll see what my genius can do—morning, he has told us, brings back the heroic ages. This is what Thoreau did, and what we all can do.

He discusses various kinds of sensuality. "A puritan may go to his brown-bread crust with as gross an appetite as ever an alderman to his turtle [soup]. Not that food which entereth into the mouth defileth a man, but the appetite with which it is eaten." A disciple asked Christ, should I give up meat? A man, he answered, is not defiled by what enters his mouth but by what he speaks.

Thoreau: "It is neither the quality nor the quantity, but the devotion to sensual savors...."

"Our whole life," he says, "is startlingly moral"—as though he has just discovered the fact. *Startlingly* registers the excitement of discovery. Which we also have made, but we don't know that until we seek spiritual realizations enabling us to ascertain that it is all true, that these moral laws are real—like a child told not to put his hand in the fire, he will be burned. He disobeys, puts his hand in the fire. Screaming, he then finds it really is true. So with the absolute truth of moral laws, if we have not yet discovered that, we haven't begun to live. Still higher and more mysterious are the spiritual laws—for the few, the very few.

We have to earn our apprenticeship through morality—the higher morality, not the received version. We have to rediscover the dynamics of moral law by personal experience, as though we are a Moses to ourselves. It won't do merely to receive the Ten Commandments; we have to rediscover and reexperience them as though they had never existed. Then we say, it is all real.

Not that these laws always burn us, sometimes they bless us. The moral can bless as well as burn, a truth evoked in Thoreau's phrase, "our whole life is startlingly moral"—conveying the idea of a man who has truly discovered it. Most people don't know this yet. Though we may affirm the truth of the commandments, to discover the universal and implacable relevance of the moral law to *instruct* us is something we have to personally experience.

He has warned us that the distinctively human quality is easily lost. Superior men, he tells us, preserve it carefully.

Women lose it more quickly then men. Although men and women have the same problems of spiritual life, their differences are significant, and woman's finer sensibility, and more elevated nature, is jeopardized by carelessness, egoism, and lack of vigilance. A spiritual man is a sensitive man, in danger of losing his quality unless he consciously preserves it, protecting himself by discipline, by watchfulness—the woman more so.

"A command over our passions ... is declared by the Ved[as]
to be indispensable...."

Self-control. You might argue that God is behind everything
and everything is God—why not give in and simply lead the life
we want? For one good reason: not all of us is divine. We have to
control the mortal, impermanent, and limited part of our beings
in order to bring about the emergence of the unlimited and the
immortal. Self-control is the medium by which this is done. If
there is no control, we are under the influence of the outer man.

> Yet the spirit can for the time pervade and control
> every member and function of the body, and
> transmute what in form is the grossest sensuality into
> purity and devotion. The generative energy, which,
> when we are loose, dissipates and makes us unclean,
> when we are continent invigorates and inspires us.
> Chastity is the flowering of man; and what are called
> Genius, Heroism, Holiness, and the like, are but
> various fruits which succeed it. Man flows at once to
> God when the channel of purity is open. By turns our
> purity inspires and our impurity casts us down. He is
> blessed who is assured that the animal is dying out in
> him day by day, and the divine being established.

Thoreau here reminds us of the Tantric discipline of India
which presents the man-woman relationship as a possible religious
act itself, rather than something to be negated by renunciation: a
yoga of the sexual relations. The passage suggests that Thoreau
would have responded to this idea... "and transmute what in form
is the grossest sensuality into purity and devotion." Sublimating
all our actions, functions, tendencies. Not denying them but raising
them to a higher level and discovering the truth behind them. Every
action, at first gross or merely physical, has inherent in it a spiritual
content, the challenge for us being to transmute it into the truth
that is seeking self-expression in this lower guise.

"... Chastity is the flowering of man." This is a difficult truth,
but if we know what the truth is, this awareness will inform our

actions at a more limited stage of development and enable us to live with what we are.

"Man flows at once to God when the channel of purity is open." We don't have to die for this to happen, we don't have to go to heaven. In fact, the mystics tell us God or the divine has no other alternative—we have the Lord in our power, we are told by saints.

Ramakrishna, India's premier mystic, used to say the devotee has the Lord by a rope, giving him control. He said that at first the Lord is the object, the devotee the pursuer—the Lord is the nectar, and the flower, and the devotee is the bee; later it is just the opposite: the devotee becomes the flower, the Lord becomes the bee, the Lord has no alternative, he must come, not only must come, but do our bidding.

It is encouraging to read that a man is blessed "who is assured that the animal is dying out in him day by day, and the divine being established." Thoreau, alas, did not achieve this but the process was well under way. That is all we have to do—to know that something is going on. If so, we're saved. If a real forward movement is under way, we can never go back to where we were, or ever truly lose the path. If an animal becomes a man, it cannot content itself with animal life again. A man who becomes spiritual and feels the surge of spiritual vitality in himself, the possibility of mystical experience awakening within, can never go back to the life of the cave. He may lose the way but sooner or later must return. Once this forward progress is achieved, it cannot be lost.

"… Nature is hard to overcome, but she must be overcome"— eventually. We can't do it tomorrow.

He remained unmarried, struggling all his life with the problem of chastity. His view of Woman is idealistic, reverent, profound. In one of his journals he remarks that he had always felt younger than any girl or woman he had ever met—even little girls three years old seemed older. He saw some ageless wisdom emanating from their eyes.

For a short period he kept company with a young woman. When asked why he withdrew from her, he replied (in his journal): "I require that thou knowest everything without being told anything. I parted from my beloved because there was one thing which I had to tell her. She *questioned* me. She should have known all by sympathy."[13]

Yet he could write: "What presence can be more awful to the lover than that of his beloved."[14] And this: "The intercourse of the sexes, I have dreamed, is incredibly beautiful, too fair to be remembered."[15]

He had thoughtfully pondered the problem of marriage, as these observations show:

> "Does not the history of chivalry and knight-errantry suggest or point to another relation to woman than leads to marriage, yet an elevating and all-absorbing one, perchance transcending marriage? As yet men know not one another, nor does man know woman." And this:

> "I am sure that the design of my maker when he has brought me nearest to woman was not the propagation, but rather the maturation of the species. Man is capable of a love of woman quite transcending marriage." And:

> "The end of a true [that is, a spiritual] marriage is not the propagation of the species.…[16] but it is the end for which the species is continued, [namely], the maturation of the species. The species [in other words] is not continued for the sake of continuance."

He may have loved women too much to have anything to do with even one of them. He was so drawn to woman's nature that perhaps the only solution for finding himself was to leave them alone completely.

A letter he wrote to Mrs. Ralph Waldo Emerson is revealing. (He had lived two years in Emerson's house and wrote the letter soon after leaving.) He had revered her as the wife of the Sage—as he still thought Emerson to be in an early period. She was fifteen years older than Thoreau.

> [You are as] a Sister.... One who is a spirit. Who attends to your truth.... An enlargement to your being, level to yourself. Whom you presume to know....

> I still think of *you* as my sister.... Others are of my kindred by blood or of my acquaintance but you are part of me. You are of me and I of you. I cannot tell where I leave off and you begin.... To you I can afford to be forever what I am, for your presence will not permit me to be what I should not be.... When I love you I feel as if I were annexing another world to mine.... O do not disappoint me.

> It is morning when I meet thee in a still cool dewy white sun light. In the hushed dawn [we meet:] my young mother, I thy eldest son.... On the remembrances of whom I repose—so *old* a sister art thou—so nearly has thou recreated me ... whose eyes are like the morning star, who comest to me in the morning twilight.[17]

This was an idealization of her as Woman, the eternal woman. She becomes an image of this for Henry Thoreau. He has no physical relations with her. He sees in her the spirit of woman incarnate. Just as we adore Christ or Buddha as representatives of the divine in man in its higher flowering. The impulse that fills Thoreau here is the same in essence. The nature of woman, as Thoreau saw it, is like the nature of a Christ or Buddha—simply unrealized.

Thoreau's favorite text was, along with the *Bhagavad Gita*, India's classic scripture the *Upanishads*. He said that after reading this text the Western outlook seemed merely practical by comparison, and even Shakespeare seemed youthfully green. These scriptures of India spoke to him at a deeper level than the great works of the West. So strong was his personal orientation toward the East that it was as though he had lived there in a previous lifetime and was now yearning for that spiritual homeland again ... finding himself out of place in the West, including nineteenth-century Concord which was as idyllic a spot as we of this century are likely to imagine, but to Thoreau it was already too westernized, outward-turned, egocentric, and loud.

In the "Spring" chapter of *Walden* there is a typical Thoreauvian sentence, packed with hidden meaning: "We loiter in winter while it is already spring." He is alluding to the rebirth of the year in his design of *Walden,* which is an emblem of the personal rebirth he is seeking. The year begins and ends with spring. The year is reborn, as Thoreau hopes to be, reminding his readers that men also have their spring. But we loiter in winter still—Thoreau making a commentary on his own life. We've got so used to our wintered selves, our state of ignorance, that when the chance for enlightenment comes we remain prisoners of what we were. The light of spring is there but it eludes us.

More than anything else, habit is the secret—taking the form of deliberate exercises. If we discover the habits that would save us—cultivating three or four—they would lead us on to perfection. We all know the power of habit—involuntarily cultivated—like the compulsion to postpone our destiny—loitering in winter when the spring has already come. We don't recognize it, as we await our transformation.

Meditation and other spiritual practices would help the mind get used to the possibility of a spiritual reality in our lives—the ideal of living intentionally, with design and deliberation, with existential passion. But without these practices we seem to perpetuate the habit of our old reduplicating selves, over and over again, year after year, lifetime after lifetime.

It is going to take some struggle to loosen the mould we are in—the phenomenon we call our personalities. Even if we are bright and educated, it is still a darkened mould of ignorance.

Intellectuals, as well as rudimentary men, are alike, trapped in the condition of ignorance.

Near the end of the last chapter Thoreau asks his readers to discover the true problems that have concerned mankind—not what is going on in other countries, but in your own. Those who are absorbed by the question of Africa or the Mississippi or the Northwest passage, attend to those things and it will be good for them. But those who have sighted the inner continent should turn to that with equal vigor. He writes about recognizing your own streams and oceans, exploring your own higher latitudes.

"Nay, be a Columbus to whole new continents and worlds within you, opening new channels, not of trade, but of thought" [18]— the thought not of the intellect, but of the deeply intuitive mind that has to be awakened as part of the life of discipline: the mind we know nothing of.

All this is strange at first. We ask—within? We enter within and find only the body and its works, the heart and lungs and so on. So sensate-oriented are we that we can't really believe there is an infinite world within. We are *identified* with the body, or at best we think that the mind familiar to us in literary reflections is the real mind, when in fact this is but a surface area of consciousness that we *call* the mind. It is when the power of the mind is turned inward—not upon things but upon itself—that the light of intuition awakens. It is not things that will awaken us, but the mind turned upon itself. The mind's rays need to be systematically concentrated by some force—namely meditation—whereby the fire of the mind can contact the inner fire, and the two fires uniting will explode in mystical experience.

The fire of the soul, the fire of the mind, fused in a consummation that makes clear in a single moment all the meaning of life.

The mind has to absorb what it experiences—not only to know there is a transcendental reality but to *assimilate* it, which can only be done through the grace of spiritual life, month after month, year after year, decade after decade, so that the moral and ethical parts of the personality, as well as the spiritual, and the physical too—through yoga exercises, for instance—will form a unity and a harmony, and we won't crash an essentially weak mind into a transcendental realm it has not earned.

The mind has to be strengthened so that it can absorb the lightning flashes from the eternal world within, and this is the life of dedication, of disciplines, of mysticism—then when the great insight comes, the mind is strong enough to absorb it.

When Thoreau was asked why he left the woods, he replied: "I left the woods for as good a reason as I went there. Perhaps it seemed to me that I had several more lives to live, and could not spare any more time for that one."

Did he attain his goal at Walden? No, but he had found a way of life which supported him in the years to follow. He had gained self-knowledge, courage, conviction. As he put it:

> I learned this, at least, about my experiment: that if one advances confidently in the direction of his dreams, and endeavors to live the life which he has imagined, he will meet with a success unexpected in common hours.

This is what happened to Thoreau. As early as twenty he yearned to live in Walden and discover himself—discover a world he was not able to find at home. He goes on: "If a man does not keep pace with his companions, perhaps it is because he hears a different drummer. Let him step to the music which he hears, however measured or far away."

This again is Thoreau to the life, a principle he followed not only at Walden but through his whole career. The mystic hears a secret music and obeys rhythms of his own. Gradually the music increases, the rhythms get stronger, and the inner symphony takes shape. But at the same time we cease to hear the music which our contemporaries are calling the truth.

We don't defy and negate them, lest they turn upon us and make our path impossible until we are strong enough to cope with them. In the early years, the early months particularly, we have to deal gently with our family and our peers so that they don't become riled at our strange ways and make it too difficult even to begin. We have to learn the art of accommodating ourselves to some extent, all along the way, to the people around us. Otherwise they may make things onerous, and the mystical path is difficult enough.

Difficult but not impossible. In fact it is the only natural path. Once we are on it we discover its truth—it was made for us, it was our life, it is what we should have been doing.

All the scriptures are for us. All the writings of sages are uniquely for those who meditate and make some attempt to become spiritual. The scriptures exist for them alone, for no one else, because they alone need such writings. Others, even intellectuals, can take or leave them and spend little of their time reading scriptures or referring to them. The sacred texts are unnecessary to them. If they should disappear, they—and most people—would not miss them.

But they are necessary to a few and that is why they continue in existence. Not one scripture alone, rather the illumined works of God-realized souls. These become essential to us, starving as we are on the food given us by our society and our age, until we find these writings, and *they* begin to feed us.

There will always be new scriptures. Even if traditional texts should die out, souls will continue to emerge from the same experiences that Buddha and others had, to tell us where they have been. As they come down from the mount to describe the experience and how to reach it, they all have a similar message.

They interpret somewhat differently because their backgrounds and temperaments are different as are their cultures and epochs, their appearance coming at varying stages in the evolution of man's spiritual history. Therefore we can't expect that great souls will always sound the same note. That would be unrealistic.

Mohammed was one of the major prophets but when he addressed himself to an uncouth savage nation of horsemen, his

effort was to lift them up from their barbarous condition as much
as he could. Supposing he had said: turn the other cheek; blessed
are the pure of heart for they shall see God; resist not evil. He
wouldn't have been listened to. Instead he gave them a doctrine
that would be acceptable, the highest they could receive. A Christ
or a Buddha would have made no headway in seventh century
Arabia with their characteristic teaching. It has to be accom-
modated to the audience and to the time. This necessity alone
would explain some of the differences in the scriptures.

Here is Thoreau again in his defiant voice, almost affectionate
at this point, unlike the first chapter where he didn't seem to care
whether he had any readers: "However mean your life is, meet it and
live it…. It is not so bad as you are…. Love your life, poor as it is."

There is something in us seeking expression and fulfillment,
something better than we are ourselves. Some presence, some
potential we have heard of. Thoreau has referred to it a number of
times. Love that in you which is seeking to expand you and perfect
you. There is something there, not merely the life of the hands—
the inner life. Love that.

"There is not one of my readers who has yet lived a whole
human life." I, Thoreau would say, am included in that. A whole
human life is for Thoreau a divine life. As he has said elsewhere, *I
never yet met an awakened man—how could I look him in the face?*
The awakened life is a life of enlightenment, of soul-realization.
In fact many have achieved this state. By saying, "there is not one,"
he reminds us of how rare this state is. Rare it is indeed but not
unheard of. Mysticism, the mystical path, gives us a chance to live
such a life.

The life in us is like the water in the river. It may rise this year
higher than man has ever known it, and flood the parched uplands;
even this may be the eventful year….

Sometimes by the shore you see where a mighty wave has
broken against the guarding sea wall, and people mark it reverently

for the future: on this date the water reached this height, the highest ever known. These massive waves are the great luminaries of the past. They tower over all others, and people say, what a tremendous wave that was. "Even this may be the eventful year." (For our own rising.) Loitering in the winter of our discontent and self-reproach, we feel it won't come nigh to us. The spring has come, the chance of *being* that wave. Five years later we go down to the shore and see where another wave has come, higher than the first one.

How would it be in a hundred years? There will be a half dozen waves breaking still higher. It is even possible that Buddha, Christ, and the others will be exceeded in time. Certainly they never denied the possibility. None said he was the ultimate.

We have much to learn. At the end of *Walden* Thoreau holds out the promise of an infinite expanse of spiritual consciousness to which the whole human race is heir. He adds: "I do not say that John or Jonathan will realize all this; but such"—that is, this enlightened prospect: the life in the water, the life in us which might rise higher than ever—"is the character of that morrow which mere lapse of time can never make to dawn."

The passage of time will not perfect us. We have to take nature's design in cooperation with our own and perfect ourselves. We have to be our own liberators. Mere lapse of time will not do it.

Shankara, a preeminent Hindu mystic of the eighth century and one of the foremost sages of India, said that there are three requisites for success in spiritual life, first, a human birth—implying that many creatures in the cosmos are craving it. According to the Hindus and Buddhists, the greatest body in the universe is the human body. If we can contemplate a life like Christ's or Buddha's, we can't imagine that they have been excelled anywhere.

In a human form we have a priceless opportunity to struggle against resistance within. The body provides more resistance, density, and innate opposition than any other higher form that other planes will provide. After we leave this earth the bodies we assume are more like spiritual, or less material forms, which are more comfortable and more refined. They do not provide the vital contraries—the resistance we need, as Blake would say. Hence someone who achieves sainthood or mystical insight in this body, in this life, has little to fear or even to learn perhaps, from other planes. No doubt he has been through their experience already. It isn't that we learn everything here in our lifetime, but here is where the highest perfection can be reached. There have been recent sages who have declared that if the gods aspire to greater perfection they will have to become men.

Gods are not yet perfect, in that they have desires to manifest power and sovereignty, and often are obsessed with their own grandeur. Only as men will they find the capacity to discriminate away the egoism lingering even in the gods, which makes them want to express themselves on a grand scale. How much superior is Buddha's compassion or Christ's intense love for humanity.

Human life, then, is not to be despised—rather to be gratefully received.

Consequently, according to Shankara, human birth is one of the three requisites. Perfection can't be achieved without it. Secondly, the grace of a teacher, or a guru; then, finally, desire for liberation, the desire to be more. There has to be a thirst, a hunger. As Christ said, blessed are those who hunger and thirst after mystical realization, which he called righteousness: no one hungers and thirsts after merely a moral life. "Righteousness" has to be retranslated to ascertain intuitively what he really meant.

Everything depends on us. We don't make the ship move. We don't make actual progress but we have to do everything that is in our power to do. For instance, a sailboat is in a harbor and has been there a long time, for months and years and lifetimes. We have the boat, we have the vast sea of possibility stretching out before us and we have the sails on the boat. But nothing happens. It is our condition—anchored there at harbor. We have to take up the anchor first of all and keep it up, because this is a strange boat: once you take the anchor up it tends to fall again. We have to make the boat seaworthy. We have to discard all the excess baggage and flotsam and jetsam, all the weight we will not need. We have to make the boat trim and spare for the long journey and we have to put up the sails one by one and keep them up.

So there is much for us to do and to continue to do, even though there is nothing we can do to bring about spiritual realization directly. We can't create progress with our own hands. The winds make the boat go, without a wind there is no movement—the wind of divine grace, forever flowing. We have to put up the sail to receive it.

This is an example of self-effort combined with divine grace. You may protest—on the one hand, divine grace and the action of the Lord who seems to be omniscient and all-powerful, and on the other, there is man so different, with his limited will—how can self-effort and divine grace coalesce? In some such metaphorical image as this. There's a place for both. Neither can accomplish the voyage without the other's help. One of the early Christian fathers said that human will—self-will—is able to resist divine grace indefinitely, so long as it wishes—a truth corroborated by many.

Self-effort—a great deal of it—is necessary. Yet without the other the ship will never move, no matter how perfect our training and our groundwork. On the other hand the breeze may come every day, every hour, but unless the anchor is up and all the other things have been attended to, there is no progress here either.

Says Thoreau: "Only that day dawns to which we are awake. There is more day to dawn. The sun is but a morning star." The sun of the knowledge that we have now—even the spiritual knowledge—is no more than a glimmer of what we may achieve later, only the beginning of our true spiritual identity.

Whitman's Self

I celebrate myself, and sing myself,
And what I assume you shall assume,
For every atom belonging to me as good
    belongs to you.

—Walt Whitman, "Song of Myself"

Walt Whitman

Walt Whitman (1819-1892) meanwhile writing his first book of poems, *Leaves of Grass,* (1855), down in New York City at this same time, comes to us as seemingly already transformed when we first meet him. In the long 60-page poem, "Song of Myself," that launches his book, he declares that he has achieved the mystical consciousness and that his poem is written out of that new mind. He does not say this in so many words but it is implied throughout the ambitious, highly organized work. Further, we can infer the onset of mystical experience by noting certain basic biographical and literary facts about Whitman:

He was born in 1819 in a rural area of Long Island, where simple working people—farmers, fishermen, seamen—were prominent in his early life. The strongest religious influence—that of the Quakers—comes to him efficaciously through his mother. The Quaker doctrine of the Inner Light impressed him—each person, he heard, contained within him a power of divine inspiration if he would grow quiet enough to listen for its voice. Creeds, bibles, churches, ministers were all secondary. As a boy he attended many Quaker meetings, and though in later years the connection lapsed, the impression remained.

While Walt was still young his family moved to Brooklyn, a suburb of the burgeoning metropolis of New York. His father was a carpenter, mason, and farmer, an alcoholic, something of a ne'er-do-well. Whitman was not close to him but exceptionally close to his mother. The rest of his large family, which included nine children, is less than ordinary—nondescript struggling people not at all interested in any of Walt's characteristic concerns throughout his life. This is a theme one frequently encounters in studying the lives of mystics—their families are often undistinguished, mediocre, so that the mystic seems to find himself among strangers from the start. None of Whitman's family would suggest the kind of career that was eventually his. In fact, mental instability was part of the family legacy.

In other words, if the household setting is too comfortable the mystic feels at home from the beginning, and is not driven to seek his truth—and his true home—outside the family bounds. This is not to suggest we should have disordered upbringings. But from the point of view of hindsight, the hunger of the mystic for self-realization—for God-realization—is so intense, so unique, that as we examine his life as a whole everything that happens to him may be seen to be significant, part of a design. His life becomes too valuable to be left to the mercy of chance, or nature, or to be understood in terms of common-sense values alone.

It is striking, then, that the backgrounds and family life of mystics almost invariably give us the sensation of the loner amidst the tribe, the speckled bird, the person alienated by his environment—perhaps to generate in him a lasting hunger so that he will feel at home only in his true milieu. My kingdom is not of this world, says Christ—the mystic's cry also. He has to find his own kingdom and he won't find it so easily if family life has made him feel peaceful, well content, from the outset.

Whitman is largely self-educated, had little schooling—five years or so. He works as a carpenter with his father for a time, and while still living at home, finds work, without delay, in printing offices. He has a natural gravitation to the world of print. At first he works as a typesetter but, despite his lack of formal education, has a gift for literary expression, and gradually is made reporter, assistant editor, and editor in a series of newspapers in the expanding borough of Brooklyn, and gains a reputation in that world.

In addition he began to write poetry and fiction for newspapers and magazines in the ten years prior to 1855. The verse was derivative, unoriginal, and the fiction too was the kind expected then: sentimental, melodramatic, commonplace. His warmest admirers have been unable to discover in this early work signs of genius, or even talent much above the ordinary. All that he wrote then has been ferreted out by devoted scholars and none of it is worth reading. Whitman himself was careful later on not to divulge too much about so undistinguished a part of his career. Likewise, his professional writing for newspapers—editorials, and so on—is familiar hack-work.

This surprising discovery becomes particularly important in the light of what is to follow.

Whitman's journalistic career continued through the 1840s and into the 1850s, while he was editing newspapers in Brooklyn and New York. He became a colorful hanger-on in newspaper circles and fell into the predictable life-pattern of a young struggling journalist in the bursting world of New York in the middle of the 19th century. He had the kind of experiences and went to the same places that others did—with a difference, however.

There was more humanity about Walt Whitman than with the others. He preferred to spend his time with simple, unpretentious people than with some of the Manhattan intellectuals his peers were frequenting. His favorite off-time occupation was riding the big horse-drawn omnibuses the length of crowded Broadway in Manhattan from the Battery up to Central Park, a distance of six or seven miles, back and forth—and he did this for years. All the drivers got to know him. Sometimes, when he discovered a driver was ill, Walt would take over the bus himself and give the driver his regular money for that day. He loved the sights and sounds, the endless variety of Broadway, of the exploding new metropolis. "What a fascinating chaos is Broadway!"—he exclaimed—"the bustle, the show, the glitter ... the gaudiness!" Happily he lost himself in the ever-changing flux, the noise, the color, the tides of humanity. Even though he was living in Brooklyn at the time, he called it "my city." When he rose in the morning he could see the rapidly growing skyline of southern Manhattan in the distance, and he thrilled at the prospect. The spires being erected seemed a symbol of the New World, the American Dream incarnate.

Though spiritually apart from members of his family, he remained close to them in other ways. If he had it, he always gave his mother, brothers and sisters money whenever they needed it. The unselfish note is evident all his life. Likewise, whenever there was a crisis, Walt was the one they would turn to for funds and help. Typically, however, he kept to himself a good deal. He was noted throughout his life for his independent spirit—another almost universal trait marked in the careers of mystics. (The determination, the strength, the daring, the self-reliance they will need for negotiating the mystical path must be present even during the unregenerate years.) He never married. He doesn't seem to have had any close relationship with a woman (except his mother), although some women came to admire him and to fall in love with him after his work became known.

His humanitarianism, his love of mankind, his innate ease with people, his inborn egalitarian instinct is perhaps best demonstrated during the Civil War when he truly agonized as much as anyone over the terrible slaughter of his countrymen. He chose neither side. As a male nurse or Wound-Dresser, as he described himself, he tended Southerners as well as Northerners. He felt they were all his brothers.

Through the 1840s and early 1850s, then, we glimpse him in a very mundane background, where we look in vain to find in his writings or in his life some incident, poem, or insight that will mark the emerging great poet or the authentic mystic. It simply is not there.

From 1852 to 1854 it is not certain what he was doing most of the time. He largely withdrew from his journalistic activities and seems to have entered a period of incubation, of preparation for something which he may have sensed was about to appear.

Emphasis has been put on the commonplace nature of his life through the early 1850s because in itself it provides powerful testimony to the transformative power of the mystical experience. When this came we don't know exactly. It was presumably shortly before *Leaves of Grass* in 1855.

This unprecedented work, published at his own expense, went almost completely unnoticed. The only person to give it any attention was Ralph Waldo Emerson, who had been, though the two had not met, Whitman's absent mentor. Whitman had been reading Emerson during the 1840s and 1850s—Emerson's preeminent period. As he said later: "I was simmering, simmering, simmering—Emerson brought me to a boil." Emerson stands as one of the major formative influences on Whitman's intellectual development, particularly the essays that articulated the Transcendental idea of the Oversoul, the divine nature of man, his immortal destiny—ideas which Emerson was the first American to embody seriously, philosophically, in his prose. Ideas which drew considerably from his own readings in Oriental mystics, from the *Upanishads* especially, which were then being translated for the first time into a Western language. Emerson became the intermediary for so many to the thought of the Orient, and was so for Whitman. At the same time, about the period of the early 1850s, Whitman had begun himself to read in these same transcendental scriptures, with their constant variations on the intoxicating theme of the universal One. In the ancient texts Whitman could discern the very source of the dazzling ideas which were so enchanting to him.

With the publication of *Leaves of Grass* we know that something happened to Whitman that brought all his simmering, undeveloped, rather chaotic personality to a head and gave him a sense of self for the first time—the self he had been seeking during the years of drift prior to 1853 or 1854. This assumption is further confirmed when we discover that the subject matter of the poem that takes up most of the volume, "Song of Myself," is one long symphonic celebration of his discovery of a new self, a new consciousness ... indeed, his experience of his own soul for the first time.

Although we don't know when the experience occurred (nor did Whitman himself indicate it directly in his later life reminiscences), we can suppose it was fairly soon before 1855, because in 1851 and 1852 he was still turning out the other kind of material, which, as we have seen, showed no mark of special inspiration. Suddenly we have a major poet emerging full-blown in July of 1855 when he was thirty-six years old and significantly with a poem that will be called, uniquely, "Song of Myself"—as though he has found what he has been looking for.

Various streams of influence had helped, such as the Quaker doctrine of the Inner Light, of direct inspiration, recalled so strongly from childhood, Emerson as well as the *Upanishads,* and other writings of the time—the various Transcendentalist writers of Europe, led by Thomas Carlyle, who were sounding new, semi-mystical chords of thought perceptible to the discriminating.

Whitman, despite his lack of formal education, had read voluminously, and made himself thoroughly familiar with the main intellectual and religious currents of his time—articulated in the thrilling doctrines of the spiritual oneness of all life and the divinity of the human soul.

Again Whitman responded to this idea ardently because of his own instinctive love of the world, his natural love of humanity. It seemed to him a powerful philosophical synthesis for what was a temperamental urge in him to begin with. Most of his advanced contemporaries lacked, to the same degree, Whitman's natural empathy with the world of the senses, and the body, the universe of things—the ordinary universe of humanity. Then to discover in his readings from the Orient, and in Emerson and Carlyle, that this feeling could be justified in terms of the highest mystical insight, such as that all men are one, that the soul was divine, and indeed—as the *Upanishads* were saying—*thou art that,* thou thyself, *in* thyself, *art* that divinity, that Oversoul that Emerson spoke of. Whitman became excited at this. Could it be true? So many of his intuitions felt in his blood, in the current of his being, in the previous years, were now consolidated, confirmed.

But one experiences in mystical intuition only what one has previously thought about and dwelled on and, usually, in accordance with the strongly marked tendencies of one's given personality. So it was with Walt Whitman.

When the moment was ripe, his mind was conditioned for what it inevitably had to receive and experience. Not only intellectually was he prepared—temperamentally also. What he felt with his senses and what he thought with his intellect were of one accord and, together, led him on to the moment of truth which he commemorated with passionate, self-renewing ecstasy in "Song of Myself."

Specifically his—more than that of any other mystic of whom we have record—was a nature intensely identified with the everyday life of men and women: a warm, exuberant, outgoing, democratic, compassionating humanitarian personality. His sense of *touch* was highly developed. He loved to put his arm around people, to touch them while talking, to mingle closely with them. Everyone knew him by his first name. Nothing human was foreign to him. Even in his once-born state, prior to his mystical experience, he was an authentic lover of life.

Hence it would not have been difficult for him to relate the electrifying transcendental doctrines of oneness and divinity of man to the feelings that had so often come over him among the crowds on Broadway and among ordinary men and women wherever he met them: a sense of some divine life operating through them, in them, and perhaps *as* them, while they remained strangely unaware.

• • •

We see that while the mystical insight is fresh upon him he writes a book unique in his experience, calling it *Leaves of Grass* (of which, "Song of Myself" stands as the centerpiece). That is, the poems will flow from him now and henceforth as effortlessly and organically as leaves of grass from the breast of Mother Earth.

He had much confidence in the work and did not hesitate to publish it at his own expense. In fact, almost all of the nine editions of the work he published himself. For the most part he never became famous or the poet of the people that he dreamed of. How appropriate it would have been for Walt Whitman, the celebrator of Broadway and the teeming life of humanity on the streets of New York, to write a momentous poem and have it universally accepted by these same people that he loved—it was not meant to be. In fact, of all the major poets in English he has been the least read by the general reader. He has always been the poet of the few. The irony that he never communicated himself, then or later, to the very people he so ardently wished to.

Because his subject matter is so peculiar. The average reader cannot easily identify with his singular outlook, his enigmatic personality, his apparently colossal conceit and megalomania—the impression many have of him when he is first read. Perhaps it will change now that more and more people are becoming attuned to the hidden doctrines of mysticism, so that he may eventually be seen for what he is, namely, a mystic. Therefore it is not the egoism of the ordinary self, of course, that is the "I" in Whitman, but rather the projection, into everyday life, of the cosmic self, the mystic and transcendental self. The "I" that he had experienced. No longer did he merely read about it in Emerson, or feel it in a dim, intuitive way, as when he mingled with the Broadway crowds, sensing "there is one life here—but what does it mean?" He had the mystical feeling often—the great love in him that went out to others ... in those years before the experience came. But at the same time his mind was dragged down and distracted by the many claims on him, particularly the claims of an impoverished, shiftless family often dependent on him.

He could not get completely disengaged from these attachments and confusions, until the "Daybreak" experience (as he calls it in "Song of Myself"), and immediately this consciousness, which had been but inchoately stirred earlier, comes into its own, announces itself like a sun rising. And his poetry now will be a succession of songs of that mystic self, songs of that transcendental consciousness experienced at last. To use R. M. Bucke's term, it is the Cosmic Consciousness that he experiences.

In fact, Bucke received this term from his association with Whitman. Bucke, the Canadian psychiatrist, student of mysticism, and author of *Cosmic Consciousness,* thought Whitman was the greatest mystic of all time. This is no doubt an exaggeration, due to the benevolent charm of Whitman's personality, which Bucke knew closely for years at the end of Whitman's life as his biographer and friend. Anyone who knows familiarly a mystic, who also has this kind of personal charm, will be apt to feel that he is unique among men. Nevertheless there was unquestionably something wonderful about his personality.

Yet, despite Bucke's paeans of praise, Whitman had limitations, character defects, which slowly grew as the years passed. The mystical experience seems not to have been repeated in later years, and Whitman's poetry after 1855 did not develop significantly. He continues to write and expand *Leaves of Grass.* The way the grass grows, his poems grow, edition by edition. Dozens of poems become many hundreds of poems and he reluctantly edits out less desirable portions. He loved his work from the beginning but it began to deteriorate.

It becomes mannered, an imitation of his earlier self. The mystical experience does not come back and Whitman *does not work to bring it back*. Which, of course, is the natural thing to do— namely, do nothing about aligning one's life with the secret demands of the realization. He went on as before, as so many have done (particularly in past decades) who have had an unusual and sometimes genuine spiritual awakening. They tend to want to go on as they have, without acting in such a way that would make their lives attuned to it and make themselves a magnet and fit instrument for its return.

This is what Whitman did. The mystical illumination does not return for the good reason that he made no serious attempt to alter his life to accord with the dimensions of the experience—its implications, and requirements. Assuming it would return, he continued on in the same way—only more exuberant, more joyous, more carefree (because now he was justified on a triumphant scale for his temperamental inclinations). There is no reference in his journals or letters to meditation, spiritual exercises, or even to prayer (except in the most glancing way).[1] He does not seek out other souls kindred to him by virtue of their spiritual aspiration, from whom he might have gained strength, reassurance, special companionship, and to whom in turn he could have provided personal inspiration.

We might compare Whitman's course of action with the response of other mystics to their own illuminations. Recall St. Paul's subsequent retreat into solitude for three years and not re-emerging until he had gained integration of all the forces of the personality, spiritual and non-spiritual, which the Damascus Road experience had suddenly awakened. And so many others who struggled for years after the visitation of truth to bring the total personality into focus with the authentic vision, to make the spiritual center that had emerged the only center of their advancing consciousness.

Whitman not only did not do this, but, according to Bucke, and to much internal evidence in his life and work, seemed to appropriate the experience into his phenomenal consciousness, his ordinary mind, and to *use* it, and the insight it had given him, to serve the purpose of that mind, the nature-given personality, known and cherished by Whitman too uncritically.

Therefore, after the early flowering in the mid-1850s his work slowly declines. It becomes more topical, politicalized, more average. He continues in the same tone but the substance, year by year, goes out of it. He writes not out of the consciousness of a changed self realized but more and more out of the memory of it. Gone is the sense of immediacy which "Song of Myself" uniquely projects. He seems more intent on preserving a certain image or persona—the Good Gray Poet image, for example. His greatest poem—certainly his greatest mystical poem—remains his first one.

Though the experience was not repeated, it provided, for many years, a reservoir of mystical insight *remembered*—from which he drew in scores of succeeding poems. He would, with often technical success, imitate the *mood* of his experience, the spirit of the earlier insight, long after it had receded. And of course inevitably mixing the recollection of wisdom with less inspired passages, less mystical attitudes, that were the fruits of everyday living.

With his attractive personality to begin with, made more wonderful by his knowledge of superconscious truth, he carries on as before. No changes are initiated. What he had been before, he continues to be. He acts as though the mystical moment was an aspect of the personality he had known from birth. Hence there was no incentive to amend his ways. His lifelong indolence, procrastination, for example, which many noted, his deep-rooted self-indulgence, continued for the rest of his life—only growing worse as time went on.

He was still a remarkable, fascinating man—charming, lovable, warm, sympathetic. But he did not renew himself. He did not develop after 1855 (when he was thirty-six years old). The glory did not return. And inevitably his literary work reflected this.

He has a good life, has many friends, writes valuable works, but doesn't *grow*. The high point is reached in 1855. The poetry then, of necessity, begins to deteriorate slowly. Every now and then he will write an outstanding poem, usually a set piece, inspired perhaps by the Civil War tragedy, which provides an irresistible background for the act of poetic creation for someone like Whitman, with his anguished love for his fellow man, or a poem on the assassination of Abraham Lincoln, one of his heroes, that is famous. There were *occasions,* in other words, that brought out the best in Whitman: short, wonderful pieces of poetry. But nothing like "Song of Myself." They were not mystical poems. They were crafted works of poetry that can be better treated from a literary rather than a spiritual standpoint, and are so treated. The mystical ambiance is lacking, the immediate cosmic insight is not there.

The Civil War passes and the nation grows, but Whitman does not. Yet he is rarely gifted, picked out by fate, by life, to be not only a poet but a seer, the announcer of great revelations, the herald of a new age. This is the kind of role he was cast for, truly; and did not measure up to the high expectations of the gods. He clung too persistently to his ordinary self, and ways … though of course the cosmic awareness remained, if in a diminishing degree.

There were a number of negative things about his life, nothing too drastic—rather a series of deceptions that surprise and disappoint us. He was embroiled in too many controversies with editors and other writers. Criticism of any kind he did not tolerate well. Unfavorable reviews rankled him all his life—not an exceptional trait in Whitman, but in a man of his spiritual endowment an expendable one, which he made no attempt to root out. He was increasingly a self-publicist, the way politicians are—Whitman's province being the dissemination of *Leaves of Grass* and the consolidation of the contrived public image he chose to present to the world. He would often write anonymous reviews of his own works, praising them extravagantly—even surpassing Bucke in this respect!

This is not to suggest that his was not a grand and noble nature. For all his defects and bravado, he was a great man. His volunteer hospital service during the Civil War alone stands as a monument to his deeply compassionate nature, his genuine love of mankind. And we have noted his unabated generosity to his mother and family for years on end. Nevertheless his personality was flawed by an ordinary egoism and self-serving interest at the same time that he gave natural expression to the other impressive, ennobling tendencies: they existed side by side in Whitman. He made no real effort to eliminate the negative traits to make room for something deeper that might elevate him to that perfection, which Bucke, in the ardor of friendship, attributed to him.

In truth we can see Whitman as a kind of prophet, a man like Jonah, called out to lead the people to a new spiritual understanding. This is Whitman's role, what he sensed, what "Song of Myself" radiates—the reverberations of the prophet's awareness of his destiny, his mission. It is what gives the poem its unique character. The "I" in that poem is the "I" in Christ and Buddha, in all the mystics, that says, I am one with the Father—*that* is the "I" in "Song of Myself," *that* is the Self Whitman is celebrating. It is not the self that wrote those bad pieces of fiction, had difficulties with his father, fabricated a deceptive persona for the consumption of his readers, and the like—but the self that emerged in 1855, the consciousness that flowered then, with which he could try to identify and *become that*—unsuccessfully, as we have seen. In reality it isn't that there's a Whitman and then there's a consciousness that is divinely experienced in addition to that. No. That consciousness *is* Whitman, and the poem "Song of Myself" celebrates that bursting realization.

As for the other, the ordinary self, Whitman, as certain mystics have, never disowns it, never says, you are ignoble and debasing and I will try to crucify you. Whitman says, No, I will not torture or even change you, I will accept you as you are. The uninspired self that goes along with our revelations—towards this he had a rather tender feeling (perhaps too tender), as though to say, come along with me, you too, because you are my vehicle, you the garment with which I am functioning—you, too, will be part of the glorious experience. I will not reject you.

For Whitman this is the body and the humble and unknowing life it symbolizes—like the life of a dog among adults.

A dog, a well-loved pet, mingles with adults, knows their tastes, marks their moods, is present in the midst of tragedies and comedies and all the crises of their family life, and yet how little he knows of what goes on in the family. The dog is like the lower self that we carry around with us—after the illumination comes. What are we going to do *now* with this self, which is so troublesome for us? Whitman's solution is to deify it, to see it as a portion of the divine design. If not divine in essence, at least divine in its function. The body is necessary for our development, and likewise the self that attaches to it and identifies with it—the humble, dog-like self.

It is a good solution, that will help us to relate to the selves of others with something of the compassion and forbearance that Whitman brought to all his personal contacts. It will remind us of the divine presence animating every level of our life—not only the higher ones. It will induce humility, decrease tension, provide a healthy margin of tolerable acceptance of ourselves as we are, on the creaturely level, without feeling that we have to transform that creature-consciousness at once.

But there are dangers and temptations in this approach and Whitman succumbed to them. By accepting the everyday self in the way that he did, he came, in time, to think of it as his whole self—what we all will tend to do if we do not protect ourselves by study, discipline, and meditation: the protections Whitman did not seek for himself.

Furthermore, if Walt Whitman had left his ordinary self behind he would have had to leave behind the life of Broadway of which he was so fond—and this he could not do. Also, one must concede, his very sympathy of outlook toward others, his empathetic compassion toward everyone, prevented him from giving up his ordinariness in any respect, indeed almost compelled him to glorify it. Which is what happened.

It was a sublime conflict that Whitman faced—if he thought about it consciously enough to realize that a full-scale conflict it truly was. Had he been able to resist the lure of his lower nature a little more, though, he would have developed the higher self, which is, after all, what has attracted us to Whitman. We wouldn't be studying him, he would not have become a true poet, had it not been for the higher experience. Had he made more of an effort to subdue his lower humanity in order to develop a more divine dimension, his life and work both would have been fulfilled.

He was in love with the manifestations of the Divine more than with the Divine itself, the Source of those manifestations. This accounts for his long catalogues of innumerable sense objects from the world of experience and imagination. In each of these particular forms, Whitman might declare, radiates the divine spirit; through each moves the supernal, the divine mystery. But to be attached to the forms *only* is finally to lose sight of the source itself, and Whitman is not the last to have fallen into this dilemma. "I lost myself," says St. Augustine, "among a multiplicity of things." So Whitman lost himself. This is especially significant, momentous really, if one has had an experience *of* that source.

We perceive there are vital lessons in a career like Whitman's— a fateful, universal existence. Any great life has symbolic lessons for all of us, if we can read it accurately, but when mystical experience—that is, from the beyond, from the divine world—is part of it, it truly becomes a phenomenon watched over by the powers-that-be.

When he was fifty-three he suddenly suffered a stroke, was paralyzed, and never fully recovered for the rest of his life. He had to leave Washington where he had been working for the civil service and go to live with his brother George and his wife in Camden, New Jersey—then and now a grimly industrialized place. Requirements of his employment had compelled George to purchase a house in Camden.

As a result of Whitman's sacrifices during the Civil War, he had been working for the Civil Service with a small pension from a job with the government, but it was not very much. Nor did his writings provide much help. He was largely supported by his brother, with whom Whitman stayed for years. In the last decade of his life his fame had increased sufficiently so that Bucke and a few others found their way to the little house Whitman was able to buy in a drab, undesirable setting of Camden close to the railroad depot.

The paralysis may have been a stroke in more ways than one. It was like Jonah being swallowed by a whale, and other prophets coming to devastating crises when they have resisted their higher promptings, when they have not, in the old phrase, listened to the will of God, or to the insights of their own soul, which are leading them one way, and their ego-self leading them another. He wanted to go on forever as he was. He wanted to have the feeling permanently that he had discovered his soul, once and for all, and he didn't want to change what had been his original personality. In this sense he was not unique, but as a mystic he was.

Once on the mystical path, the mystic's life becomes full of presences. He grows aware of realities of which the rest of us are not quite so aware. It behooves him, we are told, to reorder his life around these fresh insights, if he is one of the chosen few, as Whitman in his thirties was. In the life of a great man like Whitman, or of any man living under the gaze of the Divine, everything is purposeful, nothing is accidental. A stroke which ends his career, which devastates his life, and from which he only partially recovers, must be seen in this context.

His last years were shadowed by gloom and poverty, but lightened by a growing sense that he had found his true readers at last. Bucke and the others sat at his feet, making notes for his biography as he wrote his journals and reminiscences, bringing him some consolation. In March 1892, in the company of close friends, the end came after years of prolonged and serious illness.

• • •

There were other conflicts in Whitman besides the central one between higher and lower self, which may be seen as reflections of this prime struggle. There were sexual conflicts. He seems to have been guilt-ridden by these despite the air of equanimity and all-embracing acceptance with which he treats the subject in certain of his poems—poems that are now famous and once were notorious for the frankness of his handling of the erotic theme. But this was not actually the Whitman as he was day-to-day. In fact, he anguished sorely over the problem. His journals, half-written in code to conceal the depth of his agony (but which naturally have been deciphered by earnest scholars), show the full extent of his anxiety, depression, and despair. In particular, for several years he feels strong desires for a certain individual, a young man of his acquaintance. There is no record of his having had actual relations with him, but that is beside the point. Whitman's own desires were what disturbed and lacerated him for years.

It had started at the end of the Civil War and went on into the late 1860s and early 1870s: in other words, when he was fifty years old, and later—long after his mystical experience—it had continued. Had he taken greater pains to bring his ordinary, too-much-loved humanity into alignment with the spiritual insight that had come to him in his "Daybreak" experience, these excessive desires might have been purged, purified, sublimated by then.

Whitman wanted to go on and be himself always and have his mystical self, his cosmic consciousness, as a kind of intoxicant, a beautifying element in his work, increasingly almost as food for poetry, rather than as material for life and personal evolution. He seems to have used his experience not only for poetry but for the creation and perpetuation of a certain role, a self-image, that of the prophet announcing a grand future for These American States, These American Men—offering himself, he said, as exhibit A as to what the American Man may become. This kind of image has some truth in it, but probably too much of self-advertisement and self-glorification.

• • •

Anguished conflicts, then, continued in his life up through the early 1870s, when he reaches his fifty-third year. He fails to develop, and in fact declines—both as a man and as poet.

Hence in his early fifties the paralysis ended most of his activity and he was alone, for years. He continued to write long letters to his mother who was living in Brooklyn while he was in Camden, very loving ones in which he would say, I lie here for days and see no one, the loneliest life you can imagine. This is after his stroke. How different his life had become! But his mind was intact. He could still write very clear letters, and revise his poetry. If his mind was intact, his self was intact. What was damaged was the body and the nervous system. But there was enough undamaged so that he could reassess his life. He is scourged by this blow, coerced by it into contemplation ... into a kind of self-knowledge he had avoided during the early carefree years. But even this may not have been enough to turn his mind more inward, to reinforce the message which he yet may not have acknowledged—a second stroke afflicted him fifteen years later.

Nothing can be accidental in the life of a notable mystic. In his case, then, the paralysis becomes purposeful, a benign thing, it becomes a providential act compelling him to assert and develop that immense store of spirituality, mysticism, and insight, which he had received merely as his due.

Having inherited or been given, at the outset, a wonderful combination of personality traits, he did not perfect, did not consolidate them into a still higher creation, which he clearly saw, at least in the early "Song of Myself," was the thing to *be* done. We are not to use these sacred insights for anything but to develop the self further, and then everything we do or write or say will flow from us irresistibly, and appropriately. We express, we act, we speak. But we don't *plan* on doing things. We should plan only on the reformation, the perfection of the character. If we have been given the grace of mystical insight, this transformation of the lower into the higher self should soon become clear as our prime duty. Then our actions, our poetry, and our worldly duties will become equally clear to us—in that order.

Somehow, Whitman did not see this. Thus it may be that the stroke that devastated him—the first of several—came to drive his mind in upon itself and turn him away from his too-much-embraced humanity. To make him incapable of riding buses any more, for the mind with which he rode those buses in his twenties was with him in his fifties. It was not sufficiently lifted up to unite itself with the other mind which had flashed upon his consciousness in that dawn of 1853 or 1854, the mind of vision.

May the salient lessons that emerge from a contemplation of Walt Whitman's life enrich us and help to awaken us, not only with the genius of his poetry, but equally with the deep existential truths that this analysis of his career may grant.

The "Self" in
"Song of Myself"

When *Leaves of Grass* appeared, it marked the emergence of a major talent, an authentic new voice in world literature. We have to assume, as already noted, that some momentous personal revelation accounted for the transformation in Walt Whitman's outlook—a mystical experience—which corroborated and vindicated him at the deepest levels of his being. And his "Song of Myself" would—inevitably—be a song of *everyone's* Self.

Already Whitman is taking his place in the long line of mystics who, age upon age, confirm and clarify each other's essential teachings.

To repeat: the "self" celebrated here is not the ordinary, phenomenal self of Whitman but the transcendental "I" consciousness, the Mystical Self, the Cosmic Mind. While the radiance is still upon him he writes down his revelation.

We cannot *truly* believe in something unless we experience it. Faith is not the same thing as conviction. And conviction does not come unless we *know.* This is the unique claim—the surpassing importance—of mysticism: that truths only conjecturable by the intellect are *known* by the suddenly awakened intuitive power. "You shall know the Truth," says Christ, "and the Truth shall make you free." Not know it by mere intellect, or as we know things by sense perception. Rather to know by supernal insight, immediate knowledge, directly and mystically arrived at. *Then* we shall be free.

I believe in you, my soul....

> Loafe with me on the grass, loose the stop from
> your throat....
> I mind how once we lay such a transparent
> summer morning....
> Swiftly arose and spread around me the peace
> and knowledge that pass all the argument of
> the earth.... (5)*
>
> We found our own O my soul in the calm and
> cool of the daybreak. (25)

The "argument of the earth" refers to the questionings and demonstrations of the empirical intellect, of which Whitman has had enough. The deeper insight comes from the depths of pure being, the wellspring of Knowledge Absolute of which the self he has now known is constituted.

What *was* the knowledge that he speaks of? It is inward, the Knowledge of the One, the Cosmic Presence in every man.

He is so kinetically oriented that he must describe a mystical experience in terms of the body. This is his strength, his unique gift. At the same time it may have contributed to personal problems later—his instinctive, too-clinging physicality. It's both a blessing and a hindrance.

He believes in the soul, but "... the other I am"—his physical life—"must not abase itself to you, / And you must not be abased to the other." He tells us more, much more:

> I mind how once we lay such a transparent
> summer morning,
> How you settled your head athwart my hips and
> gently turn'd over upon me,
> And parted the shirt from my bosom-bone, and
> plunged your tongue to my bare-stript heart,
> And reach'd till you felt my beard, and reach'd
> till you held my feet. (5)

---

* All the quotations in this chapter, unless otherwise noted, are from Walt Whitman's poem "Song of Myself," *Leaves of Grass,* 1892, 9th ed. The number in parenthesis following the quotation indicates the section where it can be found.

The sexual is everpresent in Whitman. Even if he is describing a mystical experience—perhaps most then it will be present. Nor need it be apart. Again, the symbolism of the physical, the erotic. "And reach'd till you felt my beard, and reach'd till you held my feet." That is, the soul seized his whole physical life from top to bottom as though it was seizing him by the beard and the soles of his feet and *possessing* him. Something pierced him to the bone. It was this sudden revelation of his soul to his ordinary mind which until then had only been reading about such things and dimly intuiting them. Now it experiences them. And it wants to use different imagery from traditional mystical testimonies to suggest the intensity of the experience.

From the beginning he will celebrate himself as the center of the universe and of all things, for he has experienced the truth of this wisdom.

> I celebrate myself, and sing myself,
> And what I assume you shall assume,
> For every atom belonging to me as good belongs
>   to you. (1)

But he will not separate himself in any way from his fellows: they too are the center of things. This is the remarkable message of the prophet-mystic. Buddha: You have the Buddha-nature within you; tread this path and you will realize it.

Two ideas quickly appear in the poem, then: not only is his soul the center of the universe but he is one with all men outside. In fact, there *is* no outside. This one self of his is the self of every man that reads, and he therefore would like every man to know his poetry—he craved to become the Poet of Democracy, read by ordinary men everywhere (a desire that we know was frustrated permanently). In fact, he would like—truly—to have this one work end all literatures and by itself turn the tide of human thought, create a new world of consciousness—re-create the world with a single poem. In this sense it may be the most ambitious poem

ever written. That is, with this one long 60-page poem, he wants
to transform humanity, by declaring the truth of not only his own
experience but of every man's. There is no other story beyond this,
he would say: those who have ears to hear, let them hear. If we
could only read his message aright, we wouldn't have to pen any
further poems. This would be the poem of everyone. "Song of
Myself" is the song of every self, of every man. It is only incidentally
Walt Whitman's. It is an attempt to write the only poem that tells
the true story of Man. It is the first poem—and the last.

He anticipates our moods and questionings because of his
oneness with us: "I am the mate and companion of people, all just
as immortal and fathomless as myself. / (They do not know how
immortal, but I know.)" (7)

He would like to waken them up. Know ye not, said Christ,
that ye are gods. This *knowledge* is the burden of the prophet.

Constantly he must utter truths which disturb our common
sense, but which re-echo, though in Whitman's own language,
themes we recall from other mystics. In the overflowing confidence,
for example, which his supernal insight has granted him, he declares:

> [There] will never be any more perfection than
>   there is now,
> Nor any more heaven or hell than there is now. (3)

The totality of being, composed of properties of light and dark,
masculine and feminine, and all the pairs of opposites which
sometimes too quickly we call good and evil, can never change. It
neither waxes nor wanes. Only its manifestations vary, eternally
changing and transforming themselves into other forms. Heaven
and hell are part of the reality which we are. We ask him to
elaborate. But he will not:

> "To elaborate is no avail. Learn'd and unlearn'd
>   feel that it is so." (3)

That is, what is true needs no elaboration. If we know what it is,
we won't require an elaboration. If we don't know, no elaboration

could ever satisfy us. We are in fact talking about two different realities. The mind that questions is one, and the mind that has experienced truth is another, and the twain do not meet. And yet we try to make them meet, to bring them together, to have the light of the one penetrate the limitations of the other ... as Whitman does in part by the simple act of writing his poem— and attempting to communicate what is finally, perhaps, ineffable.

As a result of his illumination he has discovered that the reality of everything is different from what he had supposed. Whitman sees sexual love, for one, as symbolic of the unitive experience that has come to him:

> Urge and urge and urge.
> Always the procreant urge of the world. (3)

Not only the sexual urge. *Procreant* for Whitman here—and everywhere—means not only the urge to beget and produce children but to beget other things—new life, new consciousness, *oneself* ... produce new selves. The urge of the world, the urge of Man. Whitman sees the sexual relationship as essentially a symbolic desire for oneness that he has apprehended as mystical knowledge. There is one life that binds all persons together and the procreant urge of the world symbolizes this irresistible force in us that wants to unite and cease the division, cease the separateness, the apartness. Whitman has experienced this one life through his mysticism and of course, on the naturalistic level, through his benign and ardent personality.

People ask him questions. What about the old and the young—what happens to them when they disappear? His realization of the Self has enlightened him about the truth of rebirth. He replies:

> They are alive and well somewhere....
> All goes onward and outward, nothing
>   collapses. (6)

Death is banished after the mystic's embrace of reality. Mysticism is Life. It isn't anti-life, it is not esoteric in actuality. It is the nearest of the near. It is the experience of life. It is the secret name for our discovery of ourselves as we truly are. Having known this, it becomes impossible to conceive of death to the mystic. He can't imagine what death is like because he knows only life, filled with tumultuous energies and bliss constantly. The word *death* itself becomes hard for him to grasp. "The smallest sprout shows," says Whitman, "there is really no death." The body may drop off. But what dies? The body dies. But the man does not. "All goes onward and outward, nothing collapses." And later adds: "As to you Life I reckon you are the leavings of many deaths./ (No doubt I have died myself ten thousand times before.)"(49)—But it is the body's death to which he refers. Whitman himself dies not. "I laugh," he says, "I laugh at what you call dissolution."(20)

Filled with life-consciousness, he becomes Life itself. His is the path of all-acceptance, deification of the world, the discovery of the divine in every particle of life in the universe, as the creator of the world might be able to do.

"To anyone dying...."—he strengthens them, brings life back. "I seize the descending man and raise him with resistless will..../ Every room of the house do I fill with an arm'd force...."(40) The mystic moves like an army with banners, but not like a man of power, of the Napoleonic type of personality cultivating power for its own sake and moving in an ambiance of awakened force. The power he has realized is reflected *through* him: he is like the herald of the army immediately behind him, which is the divine realization that is his. "...I fill with an arm'd force...."

"... Lovers of me, bafflers of graves."(40) Everyone loves him. They baffle graves because in his presence they know, as he says, "I laugh at what you call dissolution." There is no death, there is no grave—it no longer exists as a reality in the presence of this kind of man.

> I am he bringing help for the sick ...
> And for the strong upright men I bring yet more
>   needed help. (41)

The ordinary sick person needs help in an obvious way. But the strong upright man is someone who has not had the mystical experience yet. He is a tranquil type of personality—moral, well-meaning, just; but he has not discovered the truth of life as Whitman has. He stands perhaps close to it—closer than the glutton, lecher, or egotist. He represents the last stage that we go through before the truth dawns on us: the stage of moral and ethical life, of intellectual and occasionally spiritual aspiration. Many who occupy even this level are not mystics, not interested in mysticism, meditation, or anything like that. They are often well-integrated, very successful, and usually very pleasant individuals. Some of these he is referring to in "the strong upright man." They need help most of all because they have come so far and yet have not begun.

Or it may mean someone who has just begun the race. His "upright" would mean someone spiritually upright who has made a beginning, but in comparison to what Whitman has experienced it is only a beginning and he needs support more than the sick or the dying man. He becomes so valuable that he must be guided, must be reinforced: "I bring yet more needed help...." In the case of ordinary men, the assistance we give them is an act of compassion to a fellow man whom we perceive as the image of the divine but who has not yet come anywhere near to realizing this himself. Some others have come much closer but they need a great deal more help—they stand in danger of losing the precious heritage if they don't receive it.

As always, he feels attuned to Nature, understands its patterns. Its beauty touches something analogous within. Its splendor finds an answering echo to the inner splendor that has awakened. "To behold the daybreak!"(24) He is impressed by the dawn, which has an overwhelming symbolism for a mystic, but—"Dazzling and tremendous, how quick the sun-rise would kill me,/ If I could not now and always send sun-rise out of me." It would kill him because Walt Whitman, the man of the people in lower Broadway in the old days, the earthy man, now becomes so sensitive that any of Nature's divine manifestations—as was true with William Wordsworth—become almost too much for him. The symbolism of the dawn is almost too great. Notice the hushed line coming up: "We also ascend, dazzling and tremendous as the sun,/ We found our own, O my soul, in the calm and cool of the daybreak."(25) That was when his moment came.

He had not given the impression of an exquisite organism, so fine that he could hardly bear the rough-and-tumble of ordinary life. On the contrary. Not that he was a dissolute; but he impressed no one as a man of tremulous sensibility. Yet his experience has changed him, as it changes all of us.

> I merely press, stir, feel with my fingers ...
> To touch my person to some one else's is about
> as much as I can stand. (27)

Whitman has the reputation of a man who had many actual lovers, men and women, almost omnisexual in his tendencies. That is part of the image he built up of himself as the Singer of the American States. But lines like this and the following passages illustrate what the reality was behind the rather public image: "Is this then a touch?"

What *is* this sense? He had thought he knew what it was. He is a man who loved people, not only to see them but to touch them, and to be one among them. He loved their touch, which is part of his impressive strength—but, as we also noted, part of his unrecognized weakness. Now with this unique experience he sees everything differently. Thoreau told us in "Inspiration": "I hearing get, who had but ears,/ And sight, who had but eyes before...." We have eyes, then we see with something else; we have ears, then we hear with a different sense. In short, perceive with a new *mind*.

All the senses become transfigured by mysticism: we get a changed nervous system, a new sensorium. And Whitman, the man of touch primarily, is dramatizing the upheaval: "Is this then a touch? quivering me to a new identity?" He becomes so sensitive that he can no longer do what he used to do. He is frightened by the discovery of the powers that are within him:

> Is this then a touch? quivering me to a new
>   identity?
> Flames and ether making a rush for my veins,
> Treacherous tip of me reaching and crowding to
>   help them,
> My flesh and blood playing out lightning to
>   strike what is hardly different from myself,
> On all sides prurient provokers stiffening my
>   limbs,
> Straining the udder of my heart for its withheld
>   drip,
> Behaving licentious toward me, taking no
>   denial,
> Depriving me of my best as for a purpose,
> Unbuttoning my clothes, holding me by the bare
>   waist,
> Deluding my confusion with the calm of the
>   sunlight and pasture-fields,
> Immodestly sliding the fellow-senses away,
> They bribed to swap off with touch and go and
>   graze at the edges of me,
> No consideration, no regard for my draining
>   strength or my anger,
> Fetching the rest of the herd around to enjoy
>   them a while,
> Then all uniting to stand on a headland and
>   worry me.
> The sentries desert every other part of me,
> They have left me helpless to a red marauder,

> They all come to the headland to witness and
> assist against me.
> I am given up by traitors,
> I talk wildly, I have lost my wits, I and nobody
> else am the greatest traitor,
> I went myself first to the headland, my own
> hands carried me there.
> You villain touch! what are you doing? my
> breath is tight in its throat,
> Unclench your floodgates, you are too much for
> me. (28)

Whitman here seems under attack, but even a Whitman did not have mobs trying to assail him in this manner. It is the mystical, psychological awareness of these possibilities that is real to him. He feels they are out there: people trying to strip him, humiliate him, possess him...."No consideration, no regard for my draining strength...." The subconscious mind has stirred into life. The vortex of all these potencies lies deep within and he has touched their nerve, their dormant faculties, and it is as though he is being attacked from without.

The world of the mystic, the inner realm, is quite large enough for him. During these moments he lives not only in but *as* the universe. The awakening of the deeper mind is quite literally the awakening of the world. But with good physical, mental, and spiritual practices this process can be integrated and controlled. Without these disciplines there is a danger of being overcome— "I am given up by traitors"—by the voices within that would betray us: the army of the ego. The ego, routed by the mystical experience, brings its battalions to the attack—its myriad of doubting voices, so that the mystic discovers he is possessed by inner traitors, by a self-defeating, self-destructive force that he never dreamed existed to this degree—against Whitman the optimist, the lover of humanity, the man of the crowds.

It is nothing to be frightened about. On the contrary, it can easily be handled because it is part of life, it is part of us. But if we don't believe that it exists, it comes as a big shock to discover, as Blake said, that all deities reside in the human breast—everything. This is what Whitman is experiencing: deities that would undo, undermine, destroy the enlightenment he has gained. They show him no respect—why should they? Their ways are not his ways.

> Fetching the rest of the herd around to enjoy....
> The sentries desert every other part of me....

The sentries—his reason, will, discriminating mind, and other powers of his new life. "They have left me helpless to a red marauder"—a dramatic rendering of this internal struggle. Here are the deities that Blake spoke of. Here is the hell within. Whitman would have perhaps scoffed at this doctrine a few years before— that hell and heaven are within. But this is a sample of it. "They all come to the headland to witness ... against me...." The headland, a jutting promontory out a way into the water, is where Whitman was drawn. The sea is the area of danger, the dry land one of safety. He allowed himself to get out into this headland a little too far from shore, nearer to the churning waters of temptation. Once there he finds it difficult to get back. The sentries desert him, but he has done it himself, has brought himself out there, and having done that has called out for his reason—where is his discrimination, where is his will? They have deserted him, they have left him helpless to a red marauder.

The red marauder is within. These people humiliating him are powers that would cause him to degrade, expose, defeat, destroy himself—nullify what he has achieved. The traitors are part of his unrecognized consciousness. He has to cope with this domain of conflict, the unregenerate mind suddenly coming into its own, with which we have to battle, until—Be ye transformed, says St. Paul, by the renewing of your minds.

The world of treachery within, egoism, doubt, skepticism, fear, and the rest, has to be dominated and purified. It is the struggle of spiritual life to accomplish this. At first it causes us to lose heart, to be discouraged, to feel that we didn't want it this way, it was not our idea. We always thought there *was* a subconscious but it is not a reality to most of us. When we learn that it is real we are thrown off balance, sometimes literally so.

This is what unhinges many susceptible souls—the uncovering of a wild, apparently tameless and treacherous power within, the world of the subconscious. The visions, fears, mysteries that arise from this subliminal stand-off, are often too much for sensitive souls of any age. They didn't know that they carried around within them this chaos. We read about it in poets and mystics, but think that in our case it isn't *quite* as bad as that. It is the kind of confrontation we all have to face eventually, the genuine aspirants being separated from the non-genuine by their willingness to cope with the problem.

If we can get past the early period of fear, dismay, humiliation, demoralization, then it becomes an ecstasy—the challenge of life. It becomes not only a necessary burden we have to bear and an instruction we have to face but the source of illumination, of all our best moments and insights. And so the chaos gradually becomes a cosmos, the zone of fear becomes one of beauty, the unknown becomes known. And a process of purification—of integration—goes on.

In some cases the discovery of this seething world would preface a spiritual experience, and the experience might be the solution. A person apprehending the chaos that he is may turn to prayer, meditation, to a spiritual outlook and receive this kind of illumination, which would then come to give him the power and incentive to master the sprawling, teeming world he has uncovered. On the other hand, the spiritual experience might come almost unannounced, as with Whitman, as with Wordsworth (although with him it was tentative). Accompanying this grace there comes the responsibility of finding out the truth of oneself and mastering it. It may precede a spiritual experience, or may be part of it— may come in its wake.

In this section of the poem the complexity of the internal world of the subconscious is dramatized and universalized by Whitman, previously the optimist and a kind of dreamer. "I am given up by traitors,/ I talk wildly…" But now he concedes he knows the truth: "… I and nobody else am the greatest traitor,/ I went myself first to the headland…." Formerly he had celebrated the glories of touch; it has become "You villain touch! what are you doing? my breath is tight in my throat…/ you are too much for me." Revelation to Walt Whitman.

He is finding truth everywhere. He would have to solve the problem posed by just such passages, and perhaps never did sufficiently. We are not so much interested in the things he wrote and did later, as what he wrote when the truth was upon him, during the few years when the glow of this experience was strong in his verse and in his life.

He embraces everything. Not by an act of will—by the truth of being, *his* being:

> In me the caresser of life wherever moving …
>   not a person or object missing,
> Absorbing all to myself and for this song. (13)

Taking everything into himself—his larger, divine self, we must always keep in mind—becoming a magnet, irresistibly drawing the truths from humanity. No one can resist him. No one can conceal the truth from him. He absorbs all. And for this song. This ultimate poem. This apocalypse, which is—he feels—to be the beginning of the true literature of mankind. A new Scripture for moderns.

What about animals? Does he include them in his divine omniscience, his all-encompassing love? (We think of Thoreau here, and the mystical Doctrine of Correspondences—the intimate, infallible relation between inner and outer. The same insight is Whitman's, as it is every mystic's.) He goes up to the animals, looks in their eyes:

> Oxen that rattle the yoke and chain or halt in the
>   leafy shade, what is that you express in your
>   eyes?
> It seems to me more than all the print I have
>   read in my life....
>
> I believe in those wing'd purposes [birds flying
>   overhead],
> And acknowledge red, yellow, white, playing
>   within me.... (13)
>
> I see in them and myself the same old law. (14)
>
> I think I could turn and live with animals...
> I stand and look at them long, and long....
> So they show their relations to me and I accept
>   them,
> They bring me tokens of myself, they evince
>   them plainly....
> I wonder where they get those tokens,
> Did I pass that way huge times ago and
>   negligently drop them? (32)

"I think I could turn and live with animals...." He envies them. "They are so ... self-contain'd.../ They do not whine about their condition." Of course he forgets that they don't realize God either: the whining about one's condition a facet of our humanity, a stage we go through on the way to God-knowledge.

Again the refusal to separate, to distinguish between himself and anything else. The birds, the bird-life, the bird-symbolism (the wing'd purposes)—are within him. They are connected with his long past, inextricably.

> So they show their relations to me and I accept
>   them,
> They bring me tokens of myself, they evince
>   them plainly....

He seems to find part of himself in animals, a mystical theme familiar to us. Each animal will register something within us. "I wonder where they get those tokens,/ Did I pass that way huge times ago…?" Am I seeing myself as I once was? "Myself moving forward then and now and forever…."(32) They awaken strange remembrances. Every part of his mind is alive now, all the rooms in his mind open to each other. Nothing is closed off. He looks at the animals, he wonders, he recalls past lifetimes, and this awakens still further memories.

He sympathizes, *empathizes* with all—because he is one with them, he sees the truth in them. He experiences everything therefore from the inside.

> Martyrs … the mother of old … the hounded
>   slave…
> All these I feel or am….
> Agonies are one of my changes of garments. (33)

We too sympathize with the suffering, we inquire how they feel. But Whitman:

> I do not ask the wounded person how he feels, I
>   myself become the wounded person. (33)

He is particularly drawn to outcasts for the reason that no one else is. We tend to make distinctions among people, of the kind which the mystic does not make:

> [I] embody all presences outlaw'd or suffering,
> See myself in prison shaped like another man.

> [Beggars] embody themselves in me and I am
>   embodied in them,
> I project my hat, sit shame-faced, and beg…. (37)

> To the cotton-field drudge … I lean,
> On his right cheek I put the family kiss…. (40)

All are integrally a part of the family of man. But this is not a mere idea to Whitman—it has become a reality. Always there is the return to the theme of identification with every form of life, experienced from within—not only sympathized with from without. To such extent, he says:

> Whoever degrades another degrades me,
> And whatever is done or said returns at last to
>   me. (24)

(Which recalls Christ's "Whatever you have done to the least of these, you have done unto me.")

He sums up:

> [Every form of life]: All these tend inward to me,
>   and I tend outward to them,
> And such as it is to be, of these more or less I am,
> And of these one and all I weave the song of
>   myself.... (15)

> In all people I see myself, none more and not
>   one a barleycorn less,
> And the good or bad I say of myself I say of
>   them. (20)

He will not withdraw, will not be superior, will not judge—anyone. This may have been his greatest attribute as a man and far overshadows his character weaknesses: his reluctance to judge, his even-tempered humanity, his love for all, his refusal to cultivate enmity toward anyone. He goes on:

> I know I am solid and sound,
> To me the converging objects of the universe
>   perpetually flow,
> All are written to me, and I must get what the
>   writing means. (20)

He is the magnet for the universe, the reason for its being, the source of its self-justification....

The "Me" here, once again, is the soul, the "Me" is—you. The "I" of the poem is you, not Whitman. It is all of us. It is everyone's soul he is describing. There is a deep writing in the universe, behind every object, every experience, every battle, and it is meant for us: I must get what the writing means.

> I know I am deathless....

> I know I am august. (20)

These are strong words. August. There is very little in our personality that makes us ordinarily feel we are august. That state would
only come about if we experience something divine—something
august and deathless—within us; then, by its very nature, we would
use such words to suggest the new "I" that has appeared.

He doesn't care who is aware of the truth. He knows he is:

> I exist as I am, that is enough,
> If no other in the world be aware I sit content....
>
> One world is aware and by far the largest to me,
>   and that is myself.... (20)

The three worlds, all the universes, are not as large to him as what
he has discovered. We find this theme in all the mystics. Everything
pales into insignificance in comparison to the infinitude of the
Soul they have experienced. After the mystic epiphany, the stars,
men and animals, and everything between become mere leaves of
this single book which is the soul's self-unfoldment. And so, we
discover, the whole universe exists to provide us with self-
knowledge ... with soul-knowledge.

"Walt Whitman, a cosmos," he then describes himself. Where
once he was a chaos. This is the word usually contrasted with
cosmos. Chaos, a world of unorganized confusion. Cosmos, a
world of ordered, harmonized energies. His spiritual illumination
has given him a sense of unity for the first time, has helped him
begin to organize the chaos within—the churning ocean of the
subconscious mind. Walt Whitman, then—now a *cosmos*.

And by his own liberation, he liberates the world:

> Through me many long dumb voices,
> Voices of the interminable generations of
>   prisoners and slaves....
>
> Through me forbidden voices,
> Voices of sexes and lusts, voices veil'd and I
>   remove the veil,

Voices indecent by me clarified and transfigur'd. (24)

Let us reflect a moment on this. Think of mankind as part of a network of filaments of divinity, an immense spider's web of consciousness—billions, possibly trillions of filaments in this web. Each filament a soul, an individualized consciousness—each of them feeling separate from each other, none of them aware of the fact that they are all one, that the substance of which they are made is the same as that of the spider—that is, the same as that of the creator. This is the condition of mankind.

One of these filaments discovers what it is finally, its relation to the other filaments and to the whole network of webbed life, and knows also what its source is—that it has the identical nature as that source. The mystic says that once this happens the whole network of ignorant consciousness must ultimately become self-realized, because that one realized soul will come back—forever and ever—until the whole network is purified and realized. Where one particle has experienced its divinity, it can never lose that—no matter what happens to it in further incarnations. It will continually return until the entire network has reached the same condition.

This analogy might explain the belief, which some hold, that it is one great Soul that has incarnated in Christ, Buddha, Krishna, Ramakrishna, and others; the same luminous personality that is reappearing whenever needed and lifting up all the world with it. If this might be true on a cosmic scale, it holds true on a limited scale. The individual soul who is liberated becomes responsible for those he is in contact with and has the opportunity to liberate others. *May the freed make others free,* goes an old Hindu chant.

Whitman sounds similar chords: "Through me many long dumb voices—" ... find their voice in him. He is that particle that has realized itself and all the other particles dimly yearn toward him, even in their unrealized condition, as we yearn towards a Buddha, a Krishna, or a Christ. By longing for their greatness we are like those quivering filaments that know their own limitations but are pining towards that particle among them that has known the truth.

"Through me forbidden voices ... clarified and transfigur'd." He purifies everything. The saint, the mystic, can do this by a touch. Sometimes by just a glance, we hear.

How is he able to accomplish it?

"Divine am I inside and out, and I make holy whatever I touch or am touch'd from."(24) He has become like fire and anything that touches him is also burned—changed. We can never be the same after fire has touched us.

Now we feel we are getting close to him. But:

> My final merit I refuse you...
> Encompass worlds, but never try to encompass
>   me....
>
> Writing and talk do not prove me,
> I carry the plenum of proof and everything else
>   in my face. (25)

How *can* he make known to us what he is? The "I" that has seen the Truth—how can we ever know that unless we have had the same experience.... If you look in his face you will see the symbolism of his illumination. If that doesn't convince you, nothing else will.

Yet he accepts seeming defeats—even what some would call evil. Everything instructs and advances him, not victories only:

> Have you heard that it was good to gain the day?
> I also say it is good to fall—battles are lost in the
>   same spirit in which they are won. (18)

Which recalls the advice of Krishna in the *Gita* to Arjuna. One's attitude to the engagement is the only essential factor. We have something within us, Whitman would say, far beyond defeat, far beyond victory: the *Atman*. The soul. Victory and defeat are petty things in comparison to that which is learning about itself through the implementation of these life encounters. I will embrace both victory and defeat, says Whitman. I will enjoy both.

> I am not the poet of goodness only, I do not
>   decline to be the poet of wickedness also.

> What blurt is this about virtue and about vice?
> Evil propels me and reform of evil propels me; I
>   stand indifferent. (22)

Whitman, like the divine power behind the world with which he has identified, sees goodness and wickedness differently than we do: as functional differences, a part of a necessary pattern of things. As William Blake wrote: "No progression without contraries." In Whitman's world everyone is advancing, heading towards an inconceivably great and vast destiny. The propulsion forward is irresistible. "—Reform of evil propels me. I stand indifferent." The "I" here is the cosmic self, the soul which is a witness to the evolution of the phenomenal vehicle that is the soul's carrier—*that* is the thing that changes, the ego-self, the empirical self. And everything helps it onward.

The passage reinforces the conviction most of us have of two centers of our personality. Particularly in the crises of life, we often feel that there is a part of us that seems to stand apart from all our works. Something that is the witness of everything, doesn't really participate, is ever-waiting. In the *Upanishads* there is a famous metaphor of two inseparable birds, of identical plumage, on the same tree.[1] One bird sits at the top of the tree, immersed in its own glory, an onlooker to the struggles of the other bird, down there lower in the tree, still eating the bitter and sweet fruits of life … waiting for that struggling bird to draw up slowly and become one with it … and to discover where in reality it was all the time. The "I" in the Whitman passage is the bird on the top-most bough, the "I" that watches and stands indifferent. The "Me" is the bird down below, striving upwards, piningly, wondering if he will ever join his friend, envying the other in all his poise, bathed in splendor.... This is the "Me" that is propelled by evil and by reform of evil alike. By everything.

He sees Truth everywhere: "All truths wait in all things." How can we know them?

> Only what proves itself to every man and
> woman is so,
> Only what nobody denies is so. (30)

The sun rising needs no herald or corroborating evidence for its reality or its truth. It is its own truth, its own self-evidence. Every facet of existence is imbued with divinity for Whitman:

> I believe a leaf of grass is no less than the
> journey-work of the stars. (31)

A grain of sand, a wild flower.... From the stars to leaves of grass, all permeated with the divine essence.

"Thou alone art," say the *Upanishads.* Hence the stars are no more significant than the leaves of grass. The same Thou, the same He, the same It, the same That is in the stars, behind the stars, behind the leaves of grass. Even a mouse "is miracle enough...."(31)

That is, anything that exists proves the reality of God. By intuition we know this; by the reasoning mind, we know it not. The philosophical mind must adduce evidences of God; it must talk about design, and argue that the world is like a watch, the watch couldn't have made itself, someone had to construct it—therefore someone had to create the universe. He sees the way the sun rises and sets, the sequence of seasons; examines human life in terms of causality; takes the scientific approach, and comes to the conclusion that there must be a divinity behind everything.

But this is only intellectual proof, it doesn't touch the man. He is still the same at the end of his demonstration as he was at the beginning—an atheist, an agnostic. It hasn't changed *him*. The evidence hasn't touched *him*. It has only affected his reason. The man himself remains apart, unchanged. The fact that he resorted to this method to approach the problem of the divine reality means that atheism or agnosticism will remain at the end of his arguments. Real atheism, real agnosticism, is what counts in the crisis, in the emergency, on the day-by-day, hour-by-hour, minute-by-minute basis. The man who proves the existence of God by exact demonstration, by logical analysis, on an hour-by-hour basis, won't spend much of his time thinking about the divine reality, because the reasoning power is in love with itself, and is not subject to influences from the intuitive center in any *meaningful* way.

As Blake warns us, the rational faculty is not capable of knowing truth directly. Only a deep, mystical experience can establish us in the conviction of the existence of God. Or at least some supra-rational moment of intuitive awareness. Not that we can sustain this belief every moment. We too have our moments of doubt. Only a genuine illumination will wipe out doubt entirely. It cannot be removed otherwise. But short of that, mysticism also includes introspective temperaments on a path leading ultimately toward the moment of *samadhi*. That is also the life of mysticism. On that path, despite the moments of doubt that we have, we also have moments of great certitude that are beyond utterance, in which we realize that existence itself is the primary claim for the divine.

In his contemplations Whitman is everywhere simultaneously:

> I skirt sierras, my palms cover continents,
> I am afoot with my vision....
>
> I fly those flights of a fluid and swallowing soul,
> My course runs below the soundings of
>   plummets. (33)

Nothing can prevent him, or conceal itself from him. "No guard can shut me off, no law prevent me." Blessed are the meek, for they shall inherit the earth. For the truly meek—that is, humble man—every door has to open to him. By *meek* is meant the God-aware, the divinely aware man. If we have an experience of the divine *of course* we have humility. So the doors open, for the door-keeper recognizes, in the approaching man, himself: "I help myself to [everything]," says Whitman.

> I anchor my ship for a little while only,
> My messengers continually cruise away or
>   bring their returns to me. (33)

Everyone becomes his messenger, and assists the realized soul. All his desires are fulfilled. Everyone cooperates—though not consciously knowing. All love him:

> My lovers suffocate me [but not only human
>   lovers: it is Life that loves him],
> Crowding my lips, thick in the pores of my skin...
> Calling my name from flower-beds, vines,
>   tangled underbrush,
> Lighting on every moment of my life....
> Noiselessly passing handfuls out of their hearts
>   and giving them to be mine. (45)

Everyone *must* love the realized soul: he is them, their voice, their future, their vindication, their hope, their destiny. He is literally their own soul manifesting to them and hence their gravitational love of him.

They are like the unrealized filaments of the web that instinctively move in cooperative harmony with the slightest wishes of the realized particle. He inherits the whole web. The meek man inherits the web—of life. "My messengers"—everyone is his messenger. Everyone becomes his lover, because the mystic approaches each person as a lover and draws this response from the individual's deepest self. There is One Man. This is a Blakean and a Platonic idea. It is of course an Upanishadic idea: "Thou alone art." There is only one man in the universe, says Blake, says Vedanta—and says Whitman. And I am that man. All the different men and women are parts of that one life. When any part of that one man has realized the truth, then the others function like parts of a single organism.

What is his secret? — He doesn't hold back. "When I give, I give myself." Nothing can resist him—or us, when we give without thought of self. "I am not to be denied, I compel..../ And any thing I have I bestow." (40) (Again remember that the "I" that compels and is not to be denied, is not the Whitman ego-personality but the higher self whose existence he shares with us as well. To be compelled by *that* is to fall under the influence of the Truth itself.)

"Any thing I have I bestow.... When I give I give myself." No sense of ownership or possession—the thing that controls most of our lives. We feel these things are mine, those things are yours. But Whitman says: whatever is mine is yours. If you want this, take it. What I have experienced, is beyond the giving or the taking—therefore you can have all these possessions. I neither lose nor gain. He gives himself.

In the closing passages of "Song of Myself" he turns from the past, the conventional, the accepted, and hails a new kind of future: and challenges the reader—who is himself still unenlightened— to reflect on his life:

"The saints and sages in history—but you yourself?" (42) People were always saying there were giants in the earth in those days: in the days of Palestine, of Mecca, of Benares. They were telling him the sages and saints lived "in those days"—before the flood. We have come after them. We are gleaning mere grains from their reapings—which seems the best we can do. Somehow where we stand is a rather insignificant lot in comparison to the great destiny of saints and sages. "But you yourself?" *I* have experienced the divine, he tells us—and you can! Taking himself as everyman, not as a special creature, and yet—it happened to me, it could happen to anybody. So he becomes impatient at times with received systems and we have to understand him and almost accept his exaggerations because of the flaming experience which is upon him when he writes his "Song."

Of course the saints and sages of history were not the upholders of received systems in their own days, they were rebels, extreme individualists, as Walt Whitman was. And their message was, needless to say, essentially the same as his: realize the divine truth which we have done, the truth which is our common heritage and birthright.

He turns directly, with vast expectation, to the future: "I do not know what is untried and afterward, [in the times to come]/ But I know it will in its turn prove sufficient, and cannot fail." Everything that exists will have to develop eventually, will have to realize its identity and function, and the purpose for which it exists, will come to know the divine intention behind its appearance in the world. It must eventually come to something. Everything will prove sufficient, "and cannot fail." We have come this far; others will come; and then we will go on too.

"Each who passes is consider'd, each who stops is consider'd, not a single one can it fail."(43) Not in this world of One Life, One Absolute Being. We recall, "Thou Alone Art." He has experienced this, has seen that everything exists within that Thou. All are atoms within this Molecule. We are the atoms. Everything must realize the truth. Nothing can fail because everything exists by right of the divinity that is its living principle. Indeed nothing can *escape* this divinity, this indwelling Godhead. It alone exists. Nothing else exists besides it. It doesn't exist somewhere and then we exist here, but there is just this One Life and we are that, we are expressions of that, so are *Leaves of Grass* expressions of One Life. And the one life is not solely organic life, it is supreme existence, in which all must one day consciously participate.

"What is known," he tells us, "I strip away,/ I launch all men and women forward with me into the Unknown."(44)

He liberates all. The family gradually becomes changed by the life of the truth-seeker within its midst and, by the pressure of his ascending struggles, will begin to sense the beginnings of their own enlightenment. But we will have to do it. It will be our struggle, liberation, and transformation that will transform them. They cannot do it themselves. They are rooted *in* themselves, in their ego-lives, as we once were. They are helpless on that level. But the gradually liberated consciousness frees them too and without knowing why, they change. In this way each spiritual aspirant becomes a savior of his fellows. Christ and Buddha are only seen in a larger perspective. The same principle holds for us. They are the models, they and a few others, of what we ought to do—and can do. The family is saved by the God-realized or spiritually illumined person in its midst who becomes for the family and their acquaintances the Christ in their lives, the God in their histories. They don't go from themselves to God. The main influence of the divine in their lives is found in the spiritually realized person, the Walt Whitman—and any of us perhaps. The divine power, the supernal grace in the world, radiates into their lives through a Whitman: "Through me all these long dumb voices ... I liberate all.... What is known I strip away...." What is unknown he makes known. What is concealed he brings out into the open, as we, in turn, will receive from those beyond *us* the grace and inspiration we need.

So the life of these greater souls is repeated literally thousands of times in the lives of potential mystics. We should not succumb to the temptation of believing that they were different from the rest of humanity. We have to see the same principle and pattern operating in our lives. The only difference is that the light we can shed is less—for now.

How far have we come? He is a convinced believer in reincarnation—the concept is *assumed* in all his thinking:

> We have thus far exhausted trillions of winters
>   and summers,
> There are trillions ahead, and trillions ahead of
>   them.
> Births have brought us richness and variety,
> And other births will bring us richness and
>   variety.... (44)
> There is no stoppage and never can be stoppage. (45)

By which he may mean, also, the impossibility of any power resisting this inexorable surge forward of mankind and its destiny.

The past, he feels, has been realized and justified in him, and indeed there is nothing, he suggests, that the future could add to what he has already achieved:

> I am an acme of things accomplished, and I an
>   encloser of things to be.

I am a world, a cosmos. Past and future meet in him, are perfected in him—in the divine consciousness, let us remember, out of which he writes and projects himself to the reader.

> ... And still I mount and mount. (44)

He looks back, he remembers, he seems to have a prescient awareness of everything that has happened to him.

"Rise after rise bow the phantoms behind me"—the phantoms of his dead selves, his forgotten incarnations—"Afar down I see the huge first Nothing, I know I was even there...."

He contemplates the vast lengths of time and stupendous powers that went into his creation—into every man's. "Long I was hugg'd close—long and long./ Immense have been the preparations for me...." (Again the explicit reincarnation theme.) How great is a man, *in truth*? The man-woman we call a person? Preparations that entered into the design of his appearance on the earth have been endless. The complexity and vastness of the creature, man, appalls us. But only the mystic knows the full extent of his nature. Short of *his* experience, we can but speculate.

Everything in the universe has played a part in his formation, to bring him to where he now is:

> All forces have been steadily employ'd to
>   complete and delight me,
> Now on this spot I stand with my robust soul. (44)

Robust because it finally knows its own strength, knows itself in all its power, glory, timelessness.

His confidence toward the ultimate day is unbounded, supreme, because based on the conviction born of experience:

> My rendezvous is appointed, it is certain,
> The Lord will be there and wait till I come on
>   perfect terms.

He refers to him as "The great Camerado, the lover true for whom I pine will be there."(45) They will meet only when they can meet as equals: he and the Camerado. Like the two birds in the tree, in the Upanishadic fable. Whitman here is the bird at the bottom who gradually will ascend. The bird at the top is the Lord, the great Camerado, who will wait for him: "It is not far, it is within reach...."

"Long enough have you dream'd contemptible dreams," he confides. "Now I wash the gum from your eyes,/ You must habit yourself to the dazzle of the light and of every moment of your life."(46) For that life is divine if you but knew it. You hold infinity in the palm of your hand and eternity in an hour. We recall his: "The saints and sages of history—but you yourself?"

"I know ... I was never measured," he reminds us, "and never will be measured."(46) But not Walt Whitman alone. It is each of *us* who can never be measured, each of *us* who may read in Whitman's "Song of Myself" the song of his own Higher and Cosmic Self, witnessing his growth, awaiting his unfoldment, immersed in its own splendor, until we come to join it at the topmost bough of the tree of evolution.

Such high realization, while high it undoubtedly is, need not be forever deferred. It is waiting for us.

Implicit throughout "Song of Myself" is the necessity of direct experience, immediate intuitive knowledge of spiritual reality, so that whatever truth there is in the world we must know it ourselves. It is there for us. It exists for us. It is meaningless, perhaps, without us. It *is* us. We mustn't take anything for granted, Whitman reminds us, from however an august source it may be. If there is an ultimate reality, if there is a divine, we must know it by closing with it, and becoming one with it. Mysticism is not something strange after all. It is our strength, our nature. It is the very life of our life. Mystical Illumination when it does come to us will be only the realization of the self we were all the time. It is this that will finally make us known to ourselves. Knowing that, we will know everything else. "What is that by knowing which all other things may be known?"[2] asks the Vedic sage. *That* is within, and the object of life is to know that divinity by experience. That is Mysticism. That is the new symphony we will hear, the new song we will sing. The song that will become for us, as it became for Walt Whitman, our own "Song of Myself."

Epilogue

Both Whitman and Thoreau made the mistake of bringing their old mentality into the light of the new path. After the first light receded—as it must in time—the old, personality-mind returned. Perhaps not quite so strong as it had been. But strong nevertheless. They did not suspect this process—Whitman least of all.

The mystical insight came to them once, and they assumed it would be repeated. Whitman believed (as did Wordsworth, and many another) that his natural poetic personality had magnetized the experience and consequently sooner or later it would return. It never did.

Neither protected himself after a genuine spiritual awakening had come. As a result they both reached a peak, then gradually declined, unable to resurrect the once-glimpsed splendor, or to know how to go about doing so.

And yet in Whitman's prime, as in Thoreau's, there was truth present to inspire and enlighten us. And it is, after all, with their strength, their period of inspiration, that we are most concerned.

After their meeting in New York they discovered that despite their differences they admired one another. Thoreau said Whitman was the greatest democrat the world had ever seen. Whitman was fond of Thoreau but disappointed at his caustic criticisms at the full tide of life he saw on Broadway: Whitman still embracing these

125

men, Thoreau finding fault with them. Whitman has seen the hand of God in their lives. Therefore, "Whatever interests the rest interests me...."(42) Perhaps this was an unwise decision. He might have loved them more from a distance instead of mixing into the moil of their humanity, reading in their newspapers, engaging in their controversies, and fighting in their battles. He would have it both ways.

Each had what the other lacked.

The ideal life would show a combination of their dominant traits. Thoreau possessed will, power to renounce, dedication, independence. Whitman possessed love for humanity. Thoreau insisted on knowing the divinity behind appearances. Whitman was content with the divinity within appearances. Thoreau lacked compassion, understanding, forbearance toward the weaknesses of others. Whitman lacked power of discrimination, and vigor of will. From Thoreau we learn the necessity of a consecrated, spiritual life, the great challenge of self-conquest and inner purification as a precondition to higher realization. His is the austere, monastic approach, of which every seeker, to some extent, stands in need. From Whitman we learn the secret (in Vivekananda's phrase) of the deification of the world, the necessity of cultivating a sense of the divine in all forms of life.

Thoreau gives us willpower, Whitman gives us humanity— the ideal is to combine them!

Each failed precisely because of the nature of his deficiencies: Thoreau largely because of the scorn for the weaknesses of lesser men, which drained his psychic energies and demoralized his attempt to reach higher levels of consciousness. For these "lesser men" were part of him, also—part of the divinity he sought to realize. In scorning them he was scorning the divine. His year-long depression a half dozen years after the Walden period was undoubtedly caused in good measure because of this unrecognized moral, psychological conflict that was so large a burden to a spiritual seeker, of all men.

Whitman failed because of his unredeemed physicality. (The strokes that paralyzed him in his fifties and sixties may be seen as divine judgment on a life that had frustrated the graces and potentialities that were his in his thirties and forties.) He clung, as did Thoreau, to his original tendencies too vehemently, even after he had glimpsed the possibility and necessity of another way of life. Thoreau had been withdrawn, contemptuous of men from the beginning; after his spiritual progress he tended to remain so. Whitman was a too-easy, thoughtless lover of humanity in the naturalistic way—almost promiscuously so—from the outset, and tried to retain this outlook to the end, insisting that what had been his temperamental wisdom, the wisdom of his pulses, of his flesh, of his senses—from birth, that is—was the highest wisdom as well. Tragedy resulted from the determined hold of this delusion upon his mind.

Thus each failed, and significantly in the very area of his strength—a strength untempered, unmodified *sufficiently*, by the insights of spiritual life.

Both were proud. Thoreau proud of his force of character, self-restraint, self-sufficiency, superiority over ordinary men. Whitman proud of his self-glorification, his refusal to show deference to any living being, any power whatsoever. What both lacked, almost equally in this case, was a genuine *humility*.

They built their lives on foundations laid before the spiritual light broke upon them. What they were in their twenties they were—with differences, but with perhaps no *essential* change—in later decades. What they deemed to be virtues were conceptions of their unillumined minds, and had to be abandoned, along with their vices, before a true foundation could be laid. "Except the Lord build the house, they labor in vain that build it." (*Psalms* 127: 1) But they were not abandoned and thus became, in their turn, something very close to spiritual *vices*. For Whitman his body, his sense life, his ego-identification with body consciousness, was the dearest of the dear; for Thoreau the awareness of his own austere power to renounce, to will, to subdue his senses, was *his* heart's delight. For one it was an idolatry of the senses, for the other an idolatry of the will. And each paid a high price for his idolatry.

And yet we can learn much from both, gain inspiration, reassurance, confirmation of our spiritual impulses, from pondering their best work written in their best years—leaving other aspects of their story to the psychologist and the biographer. By combining the finest qualities of each—Thoreau's power of renunciation, his single-mindedness, his will, his rigor, his love of discipline, and Whitman's broad, all-loving humanity, his deep compassion for all forms of life—we can create in our minds, and thus the possibility of creating in our characters, an ideal type of person and move gradually toward implementing such an ideal in our lives—the personality we crave to be in order to reflect the inner and constant demands of the soul upon us.

Notes and References*

Henry David Thoreau

1. Henry D. Thoreau, *Journal*, Vol. 1, ed. John C. Broderick et al., (Princeton: Princeton University Press, 1981), 296
2. Ibid., 245
3. Ibid., 290
4. Ibid., 327
5. Ibid., 350
6. Henry D. Thoreau, *Walden*, "Higher Laws"
7. *Journal*, Vol. 1, 299, for this and the following three quotations
8. Henry David Thoreau, *Collected Poems of Henry Thoreau*, ed. Carl Bode, (Baltimore: John Hopkins Press, 1964), 231
9. Henry David Thoreau, *The Writings of Henry David Thoreau, A Week on the Concord and Merrimack Rivers*, (Cambridge: Riverside Press, Houghton Mifflin, 1906) "Monday," 182
10. Ibid., "Friday", 408
11. *Walden*, "Economy" chapter, for quotations in this paragraph and the following two pages
12. *Plato's Republic*, Book VII
13. *Walden*, "Economy" chapter, for this and following two quotations
14. *Journal*, Vol. 1, 289
15. *Walden*, "Economy" chapter for this and next two quotations

The Quest – Walden

1. *Journal*, Vol. 1, 296
2. Ibid., 347
3. *Walden*, "Economy"
4. Ibid.
5. Ibid. for both quotations in this paragraph

---

* Because this is a posthumous publication, a full bibliographic listing is not available. Needless to say, the author was familiar with the main biographies and written works of Whitman and particularly Thoreau, one of the subjects of his doctoral thesis.

6. *Walden,* "Where I Lived, What I Lived For" chapter for quotations in this paragraph and the next six quotations

7. *Walden,* "Sounds"

8. Ibid.

9. *Walden,* "Brute Neighbors"

10. *Walden,* "Winter Animals"

11. *Walden,* "Solitude" chapter, for this and following two quotations

12. *Walden,* "Higher Laws" chapter for this and the quotations on the following four pages

13. Henry David Thoreau, *Early Essays and Miscellanies,* ed. Joseph J. Moldenhauer and Edwin Moser, with Alexander Kern (Princeton: Princeton University Press, 1975), 271

14. Ibid., 275

15. Ibid., 277

16. *Journal,* Vol. III, 7

17. Henry David Thoreau, *Correspondence,* ed. Walter Harding and Carl Bode (New York: New York University Press, 1958), 103

18. *Walden,* "Conclusion" chapter for this and the remaining quotations in this chapter

Walt Whitman

1. As far as we know Whitman did not engage in regular, daily spiritual exercises that are being referred to here, but there is evidence that he practiced some form of mental exercises and meditation as noted in V. K. Chari's *Whitman in the Light of Vedantic Mysticism,* (Lincoln: University of Nebraska Press, 1964), 105–107

The "Self" in "Song of Myself"

1. Mundaka Upanishad

2. Ibid.

Note: All the quotations in this chapter, unless otherwise indicated, are from Walt Whitman's, *Leaves of Grass,* 1892, 9th Edition, "Song of Myself." The number in parenthesis following a quotation cites the section where it can be found.

If a quotation does not have a number directly following it, and was not previously mentioned, the next number listed in a subsequent quotation will be its source.

Index

A

Abolition, 28
Alexander the Great, 51
"Auguries of Innocence" (Blake), 2n
Augustine, St., 91

B

Bhagavad Gita, 29, 53, 66, 114
Blake, William, 1, 10, 16, 17, 21, 31,
    35, 47, 53, 59, 73, 106, 115,
    117, 118
    Doctrine of Correspondences,
      58–59, 108
Broadway, 22, 84, 103, 125
Bucke, R. M., 85, 86, 88, 89, 92
Buddha, 35, 38, 47, 51, 52, 54,
    66, 70, 71, 72–73, 89, 98
    Eightfold Path, 34–35
    role as divine incarnation, 113,
      121
Bunyon, John, 42

C

Camden, N.J., 91–92, 94
Carlyle, Thomas, 82
Catherine of Siena, St., 40
Chateaubriand, 16
Christ, 17, 26, 38, 39, 46, 47,
    54, 55, 61, 66, 71, 72–73,
    78, 89, 96, 99, 111
    role as divine incarnation, 35–
      36, 113, 121
    view of family, 32–33

Christianity, 40
Concord, 8, 22, 27, 30, 33, 42, 45,
    67, 129
Cosmic Consciousness (Bucke), 85

D

Depression, 12, 52
    and spiritual life, 11–14, 22,
      37–38, 40–41
Doctrine of Correspondences, *See*
    Blake, William

E

Emerson, Mrs. Ralph Waldo, 65
Emerson, Ralph Waldo, 12, 15, 19,
    21, 28, 29, 33, 65–66, 84
    as Transcendentalist, 16, 18, 56
    relationship with Thoreau, 2,
      7–11
    role in Whitman's life, 2, 81–83

F

Family, role in life of spiritual
    aspirant, 30–33, 70, 78, 120–
    121
Francis of Assisi, St., 34, 54

G

Gandhi, 47, 51, 52
Gibran, 47
Gita, 114. *See also Bhagavad Gita*
Goethe, 16

131

About the Author

PAUL HOURIHAN, teacher and mystic, was born, raised, and educated in Boston where he earned a doctorate in English literature from Boston University. For 15 years he taught dozens of courses and gave innumerable lectures on the subjects of great mystics and mysticism in Ontario, Canada. For over 45 years he was committed to the spiritual path and a serious student of the world's spiritual traditions, particularly India's Vedanta philosophy.

In the closing period of his life he began, at long last, to publish his compelling works. This is the fourth of a dozen books on varying subjects, but all with underlying spiritual themes.

He lived with his wife, Anna, in Northern California, where she continues to carry on his work.

VEDANTIC SHORES PRESS is dedicated to publishing the spiritual works of Paul Hourihan. Our goal is to help readers reach new shores of spiritual consciousness.

Our creative biographies, novels and non-fiction books, which incorporate Dr. Hourihan's insights from many years of meditative practice, give a clear vision and practical understanding of spirituality and mysticism based on the ancient Indian philosophy of Vedanta.

We are interested in our readers' views. If you'd like to comment on *Mysticism in American Literature: Thoreau's Quest and Whitman's Self* or would like more information on our books and audio products, please visit our website:

http://www.VedanticShoresPress.com

Or contact us at:

Vedantic Shores Press
P.O. Box 493100, Redding, CA 96049
Tel: 530/549-4757   Fax: 530/549-5743
Toll-free: 866/549-4757 (U.S. only)
E-mail: info@vedanticshorespress.com

Other Books by Paul Hourihan:

Ramakrishna and Christ, The Supermystics:
  New Interpretations

The Death of Thomas Merton, A Novel:
  A Confessional Portrayal of the Last Day in the Life of the
  Famous Catholic Monk and Writer

Bill W., A Strange Salvation:
  A Biographical Novel Based on Key Moments in the Life of
  Bill Wilson, the Alcoholics Anonymous Founder, and a
  Probing of His Mysterious 11-Year Depression